Getting the Go-Ahead:
Using Statistical Analysis
To Maximize Your Business Plans

Yoshiki Kashiwagi

Getting the Go-Ahead:
Using Statistical Analysis To Maximize Your Business Plans

Translator: Shizuka Hyogo Chien
Editorial Coordinator: Jeffery Mazziotta
Coordinator: Junko Rodriguez
Cover Image designed by vectorjuice / Freepik

Published by Babel Press U.S.A.

ISBN: 978-0-9914789-6-5

Babel Corporation
1833 Kalakaua Avenue, Suite 208,
Honolulu, Hawaii 96815, US

Introduction

"A good businessperson is good with numbers."

Many people believe this, and they have emphasized this countless times. Yet, it is still challenging to utilize data in our day-to-day business activities. We need to process numerical data to discover new information, but we often don't know *how*. This processing is done with statistics and data analysis.

Wouldn't it be nice if it were easier to utilize statistics or data analysis more effectively? Many of you may have already tried reading books and given up on understanding or applying the methods therein.

Although there are so many different methods that it is impossible to cover all of them, the methods used in ordinary business activities are very limited (unless you have a highly specialized job). It is wiser and more efficient to focus on practical methods and learn how to use them effectively.

Thus, this book will start off with widely known methods such as calculating the **average**, and end at **regression analysis**. Most analyses can be done instantly with Microsoft Excel.

This book will show you how to:
1. Get to the next step after collecting data;
2. Use the data effectively after obtaining the analysis results; and
3. Make a convincing argument (tell a story) by connecting the dots between the analyses.

Throughout this book, I'll explain how to use numerical data through an example of a business plan. Please note, however, that this is not a guide on how to prepare a business plan itself.

I hope this helps you take your first step towards becoming a businessperson who is good with numbers.

April, 2013

Yoshiki Kashiwagi

Getting the Go-Ahead: Using Statistical Analysis To Maximize Your Business Plans

Table of Contents

Preface

Ideas and Tips on Data and Statistical Analysis

Chapter 1

Effective Ways to Collect and Analyze Data

Chapter 2

How to Estimate Profit

Chapter 3

How to Estimate Risk

Chapter 4

What is the Success Factor?

Chapter 5

Setting the Target Value to Reach Your Goal

Chapter 6

Present Your Numerical Data With a Message

Epilogue   195

Discussion and Concluding Remarks

Preface

Ideas and Tips on Data and Statistical Analysis

How to Use Numbers and Data

Alex worked hard to find a job in a competitive job market and was hired at a major trading company. He has worked at the company for two years, and does not want to be treated like a rookie anymore.

However, the cyclonic vacuum cleaner which Alex has been selling has lost its popularity, and domestic sales have been plummeting. As a possible solution, the company and the manufacturer are considering entering into emerging markets in Asia. Alex's boss told Alex to come to her office.

Boss: "In one month, we need to give a proposal to the manager of the Overseas Sales Department on entering Asian markets. Can you draft a business plan? In my opinion, Country X has the most potential because it's been growing rapidly in the last few years. We need to convince the board with this plan so that they will give us the go-ahead. I need you to bring me a rough draft in two days. This is crucial for the management decisions of the board. Make sure you include some data analysis. I'm looking forward to it!"

This was Alex's first time working in international sales. Although he felt a little nervous, he was very excited.

Alex: "Okay. First, I need to collect information. Hmm..."

Alex collected the company's sales data in the domestic market at his office, and also collected online data of the global consumer electronics market size. Once he was done collecting data, he looked out the window and noticed that it was already dark. Alex felt lost with a big pile of research material in front of him.

Alex: "What do I do next? Do I just combine everything into one file?"

The next day, Alex picked up some news articles and numerical data that looked relevant and laid them out, but he couldn't find a strong link between each piece of information. It just looked like he was trying to create a scrapbook of random information. Alex was running out of time and starting to panic.

Alex: **"Use the numerical data to create a plan...How do I turn this into a 'proposal'?"**

The more he panicked, the more confused he got, and the clock kept ticking. Alex asked his Boss for some advice.

Alex: "I gathered all kinds of information, but I don't know what to do next..."

Boss: "What statement are you trying to make using that information?"

Alex: "Um...I thought I might come up with something once I had the information."

Boss: "That's going to take forever. You won't be able to make a proposal if you keep losing your way. What is your message? What kind of evidence do you need to support your message? Did you think about it before getting started? You're doing it backwards. Are you familiar with **'hypothesis testing'**?"

Alex: "Hypothesis testing???"

Boss: "Yes. First, state your main objective. Next, create your hypothesis based on your objective, and use data to test your hypothesis scientifically."

How to Use Numbers in the First Place

Thinking patterns are more important than analysis methods.

How to be Good at Data Analysis

Why are some people good at data analysis while others aren't? Will you be an expert who can produce faster and better analysis results if you learn more analysis methods?

Although I do know various analysis methods, accumulating knowledge or learning different methods doesn't directly lead to better work performance. It's more important to acquire a **good data and numbers competency (being able to use effective strategies)** and **useful thinking patterns (ways of thinking)** through adequate experience by applying data analysis in different situations on a case-by-case basis.

Reading examples of application will not prepare you for real life situations right away. However, it doesn't help to keep trying hundreds of times aimlessly, either.

As you look into patterns and approaches in analysis, you'll find that they work differently in each case. Nevertheless, there are also some common ways of thinking. Focus on learning these basic rules, and you'll be able to connect the dots between your actual work assignment and the analysis methods to be applied.

Is your analysis understandable and convincing to the audience?

In general, there aren't a lot of analysis methods used in business (unless you are an expert in analysis). The more complicated your analysis is, the more accurate it may be; however, it will no longer be versatile in applying to different cases. The amount of time and knowledge required for the analysis would also increase significantly. I asked 60 managers from different manufacturers the scope of knowledge required in the statistical methods which they use in their day-to-day business. They answered that <u>the most difficult method which you need to understand is regression analysis. Thus, everything you need is covered in this book</u>.

Even if you work hard and learn complicated analysis methods, most people who you show the analysis to wouldn't understand anyway, and may confusingly ask you "why the numbers lead to such a conclusion". Thus, you could fail to deliver your message. In real life, there's always an audience, and your presentation needs to be <u>understandable and convincing to the audience</u>.

Don't try to learn every existing analysis method. <u>Focusing only on the most effective methods and patterns of thinking</u> is the easiest and most feasible way to master analysis.

Fig. 0-1 Learning and Utilizing Various Analysis Methods vs Delivering a Message

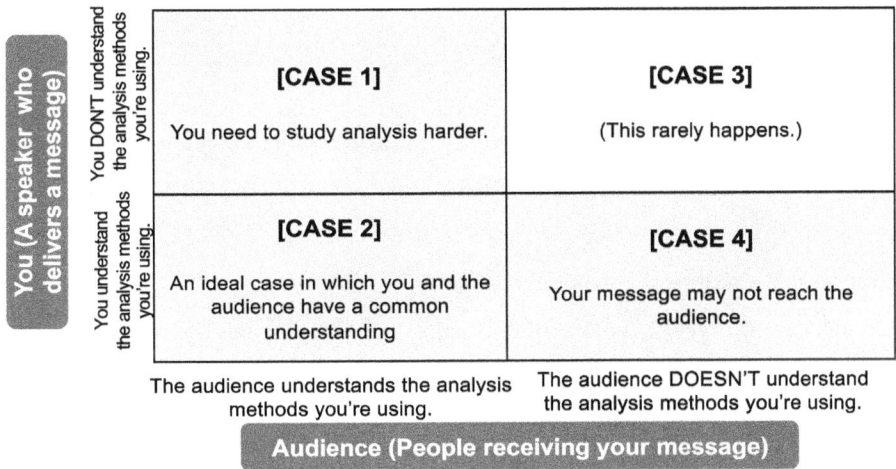

		The audience understands the analysis methods you're using.	The audience DOESN'T understand the analysis methods you're using.
You (A speaker who delivers a message)	You DON'T understand the analysis methods you're using.	**[CASE 1]** You need to study analysis harder.	**[CASE 3]** (This rarely happens.)
	You understand the analysis methods you're using.	**[CASE 2]** An ideal case in which you and the audience have a common understanding	**[CASE 4]** Your message may not reach the audience.

Audience (People receiving your message)

> # The hypothesis approach takes you from your initial question to analysis.

In this chapter, I will explain **the hypothesis approach**, which is an important **pattern of thinking** commonly used in any case of problem solving.

The hypothesis approach is effective in data analysis, because it connects the dots between your objective and the data analysis methods to be used. It will prevent you from drowning in a large amount of data and various analysis methods, or getting stuck before moving to the next step.

The hypothesis approach is widely used in problem solving in general. In data analysis, it is extremely useful in identifying the required data and the suitable analysis method, as well as keeping your analysis on course to reach your objective.

Start by guessing.

Say, your customer files a complaint that product delivery is too slow. You would surely start by listing reasons which may be causing the delay.

Here are some actions that you might take:
- Ask the employee in charge of packaging and shipping out the product
- Check past delivery records
- Investigate issues with the delivery driver
- Investigate complaints from other customers or employees

Think for a minute about how you came up with these options. You were able to guess what might be causing the problem according to your past experience, instinct, and use of common sense. Such ideas are called **hypotheses**, or, in simpler terms, **educated guesses** to reach your objective.

Use numerical data to verify your hypothesis.

As a hypothesis is only a guess, you need to confirm (verify) your hypothesis. Hypotheses have certain characteristics. In the case above, delay in packaging and shipping preparation and delay in delivery after shipping out the products are some of the characteristics. Once you clarify these characteristics, each hypothesis can be verified with data analysis.

You can take a different approach depending on the hypothesis. If there could be an issue with the person preparing the shipments, you could compare the processing speed (numbers of shipments made by each employee). If your concern is regarding the delivery system, you could compare the current delivery speed with previous ones. By analyzing these numbers, you can draw objective conclusions and convince your audience whether the hypothesis is spot on, dead wrong, or needs further investigation.

Thus, your first important step is to <u>form a hypothesis linked to the objective of your analysis</u> (*"I want to achieve..."/"I need to know..."*). Once you form this hypothesis, you'll be able to determine the procedures and information necessary to achieve your objective.

While using the hypothesis approach, <u>the goal of analysis is to check (verify) the hypothesis</u>.

If you're stuck at the first step and can't start your analysis, take a deep breath and clarify your objective. *What do you want to achieve? What information do you need?* You may not have a clear understanding, or your thoughts may be all over the place.

Clarify your objective and choose your analysis method.

Here's a more detailed example.

Suppose that you have data showing last month's sales figures (3,000 units were sold).

It's pointless to calculate the average sales unless you have an objective or a hypothesis.

Say, sales were higher in February compared to previous months. You may want to know *why*. One reason might be due to discounted pricing. Your objective would be to figure out how much sales was boosted by this discount. In this case, calculating the average sales is useful.

To achieve this objective, you would form a hypothesis that you would see a difference in monthly sales due to a price discount when you compare the sales data of February, January and last year. That will take you to the next step (analysis): calculating the average sales for February and previous months to roughly compare the figures. Think logically how you can get from step 1 (setting your objective) to step 3 (choosing your analysis method).

Set Your Objective→ Form Your Hypothesis→ Choose Your Analysis Method

Follow these steps in your head so that you won't get stuck when you choose your method or lose sight of your objective.

Three Reasons Why You Need a Hypothesis

Here are the advantages in using the hypothesis approach.

1.   You can avoid wasting time and energy on unnecessary analysis.

Decide what to investigate to narrow down the kind of data you need and the suitable analysis method. Save the time and energy that would otherwise be wasted on unnecessary or repeated work. Instead, allocate the conserved time and energy toward doing several types of analysis, which will give your final output more accuracy (better quality).

2.   You can clarify your objective for the analysis.

No matter how clear and accurate your analysis results turn out to be, it is meaningless if it does not suit your objective. When you are overwhelmed with numbers and are focused on analysis, you may forget what the analysis is for and just end up chasing numbers. The real goal is being switched to analyzing per se.

Say, you wanted to identify the reason why there is a decline in sales figures. You went through a product's sales data and finally drew a conclusion that "the consumer behaviors of men in their thirties and women in their twenties were similar." This analysis may have been nicely done, but it may not help you achieve your initial goal: to identify the reason for the decline in sales.

3.   You can look from a larger perspective.

A hypothesis indicates the factors for achieving your goal.

If you need to identify the reason for the decline in sales, you can look from different angles (perspectives) by forming different hypotheses, such as those on products, stores, or the whole market. By combining your analysis results for each hypothesis, you can make a convincing argument (tell a story) from multiple perspectives and a comprehensive perspective for the same objective.

Risks in the Hypothesis Approach

Here are some things to watch out for when you use the hypothesis approach.

- **Risk #1: You might overlook important information.**

The hypothesis approach always starts off with an objective or a question. Some very important or useful information may be hidden in the data, but without being able to form the right hypothesis at the very beginning, you could miss the opportunity to discover that information.

The comprehensive approach is the complete opposite of the hypothesis approach. In the comprehensive approach, all data is thoroughly analyzed without setting an objective or asking a question. Obviously, this would take extra time and effort, but you might discover new information which you would not have expected to find.

The hypothesis approach focuses only on things related to your objective (which pop up in your head as hypotheses), and thus the scope of your analysis will be limited. Even though this steers you in a particular direction, you may overlook something very important.

Fig. 0-2 Analysis flow

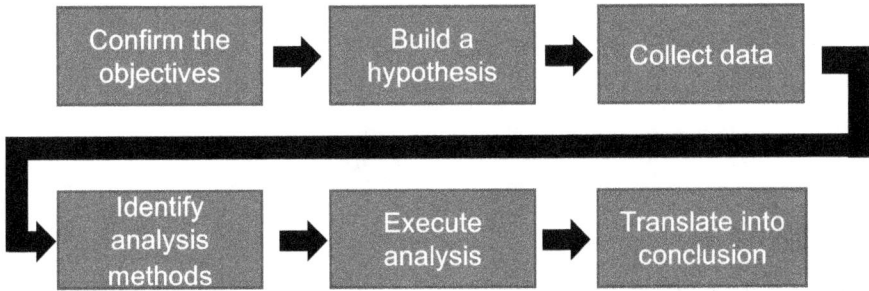

```
┌─────────────┐    ┌─────────────┐    ┌─────────────┐
│ Confirm the │ ▶  │ Build a     │ ▶  │ Collect data│
│ objectives  │    │ hypothesis  │    │             │
└─────────────┘    └─────────────┘    └─────────────┘

┌─────────────┐    ┌─────────────┐    ┌─────────────┐
│ Identify    │ ▶  │ Execute     │ ▶  │ Translate   │
│ analysis    │    │ analysis    │    │ into        │
│ methods     │    │             │    │ conclusion  │
└─────────────┘    └─────────────┘    └─────────────┘
```

- **Risk #2: Risk of Bias**

A hypothesis is a random idea which pops up in your head before being tested. A hypothesis is based on your subjective view, and there is always the risk that your assumption or bias affects your idea.

For instance, if you're investigating why there was a decline in sales, you may develop a hypothesis focused only within your own company (issues with products, stores, etc.), missing any fundamental issues such as how competitors' products or the shift in the whole industry affect the sales of your products.

Even if you learn how to analyze data in such ways as shown in **Figure 0-2**, if you can't forming the right hypothesis beforehand, you may not be able to collect appropriate data or choose the best analysis method (you may even end up with the wrong input). As a result, the quality of the final output (The "conclusion" box in **Figure 0-2**) may turn out very low.

You could limit the goal of your analysis to verifying the hypothesis, especially if your assumption is too strong or you are overconfident, and you may ignore any data that contradicts the hypothesis. You might repeat the analysis until you draw a conclusion that verifies the hypothesis, and in some cases, even force yourself into believing that the data is incorrect.

You may not even realize your own bias and carry on. This is called **confirmation bias**, and it is one of the most common psychological pitfalls. However, you can avoid this risk by learning about confirmation bias and making sure that you are not guilty of it. Be really careful. Confirmation bias may appear at different stages, including data collection, analysis, and finally, when you draw a conclusion.

Four Effective Ways to Get from the Hypothesis Stage to the Analysis Stage

Forming a hypothesis is an important step to take before your analysis. How, then, can you form a good hypothesis?

1.　Mutually Exclusive and Collectively Exhaustive (MECE)

You may overlook an important point of view if your scope is too narrow in forming a hypothesis. Having an overlap in your hypothesis could also lead to unnecessary analysis. You should avoid these risks at the beginning. One thing you can do is to use personal knowledge and experience (yours and those of others), and to use an existing framework. For instance, you could use the four Ps (Product, Price, Place, and Promotion) or the 3C model (Customer, Company, and Competitor) which are well-known in marketing.

In the section "The hypothesis approach takes you from your initial question to analysis," I showed an example in which product delivery was too slow. Hypotheses were formed while imagining every step in product sales: **manufacturing→shipment→distribution (delivery)→customer**. You won't forget any steps if you draw a flow chart instead of listing things out randomly.

On the other hand, be careful about the balance. Don't use MECE all the time. Don't be rigid in putting everything into the four Ps framework (That's not your ultimate goal). For example, if you want to form a hypothesis to improve sales, you shouldn't focus on things which you can't change or control about your product (or things which wouldn't have a strong influence on sales). Focus on things that need to be more prioritized to form your hypothesis.

Make references to the framework and check whether your scope is missing any important points before you prioritize and narrow down the scope.

2. Don't give up too soon due to current obstacles.

Be flexible and try not to exclude a hypothesis too early due to obstacles such as not having the data at hand, not having any experience in a certain field of research, not having anyone in the office with the right expertise, or not working in that area of business. Ask yourself if anything can be done. Perhaps you can do new research or purchase data or information from outside your company.

3. Think of several hypotheses.

There could be several reasons causing the issue or opportunity that your company is experiencing. If you want to make a convincing statement to your audience, you should form several hypotheses from different points of view which complement each other instead of relying on just one path.

4. Don't be a perfectionist.

It's good to have a hypothesis that is straight to the point (leading you to the answer efficiently), but trying too hard to perfect your hypothesis at the beginning could stop you from expanding your ideas, and you could end up making assumptions. Always keep in mind that a hypothesis doesn't have to be perfect.

Pyramid Structure in Hypothesis Testing

Now that you've formed your hypothesis, next, you'll need to think of the analysis method to confirm (verify) your hypothesis.

The pyramid structure is a commonly used framework in thinking of ways to analyze data based on your hypothesis. In order to get to the next step of data analysis, you need to ask yourself <u>what statement needs to be made in order to prove that the hypothesis is correct (or incorrect)</u>.

Figure 0-3 takes this into consideration along with the previous flow chart: **Objective→Hypothesis→Analysis Methods**. This is just a rough idea. In some cases, you may need to think of several steps to be taken within the "Analysis Methods" stage. Always make sure that there's a proper connection between the layers ("A is necessary to achieve B.").

Once this is complete, you only need to select the data and analysis method necessary.

Present the flow and comprehensiveness of your logic using the pyramid structure along with each analysis result. This is a great presentation technique. You can also prove that "I have idea A" and that "I analyzed idea A from different angles." It will show that your analysis result and message is credible and will satisfy your audience.

The Analysis to Build a Hypothesis and the Analysis to Verify Your Hypothesis

Most books on the problem solving approach using the hypothesis testing method tell you to go through trial and error until you prove your hypothesis: Step 1: Build your hypothesis. → Step 2: Verify. → Repeat Steps 1 and 2. That is theoretically correct, but for businesspersons, there is a limit to the amount of time available before reaching an output. In my actual work experience, I hardly had the time to repeat the trial and error process because it is a "hit-and-miss affair."

Fig. 0-3 An example of the Pyramid structure

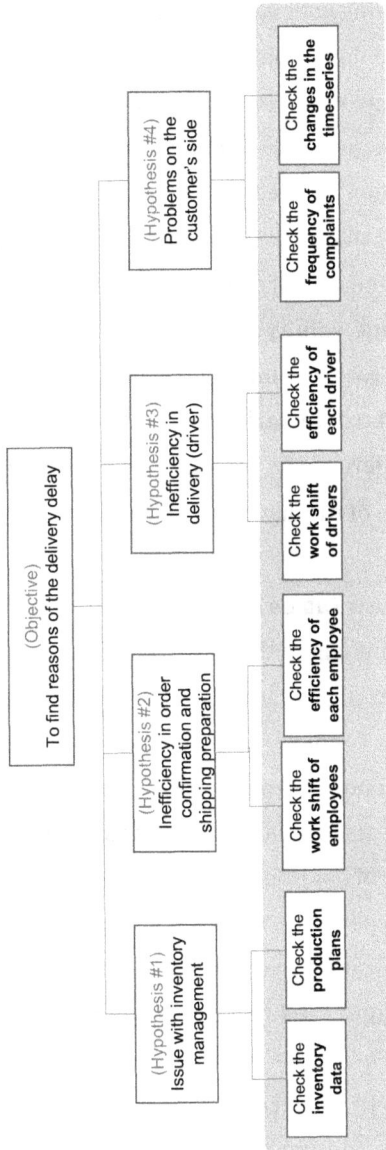

Is there a better way to make a good guess that is spot on, and move on to analyze more efficiently within a limited amount of time? This is crucial for people that are always fighting time pressure. In these situations, analysis will help you. You can improve the efficiency of an analysis by doing a rough analysis within a short amount of time, finding out from the analysis results what you need to look into further, and prioritizing your hypothesis. You need to prioritize from an objective point of view: not randomly, but based on the analysis results.

Let's use the same example: a delay in the delivery of products. There are four different factors to consider in forming your hypothesis: manufacturing, shipment, delivery (distribution), and customer. Say, you want to do a rough analysis on the work performance of the delivery driver (distribution). You can quickly try the following (I'll show you the details of analysis in the following chapters.):

- Compare **the average values** of the current and past delivery time. You may discover roughly at which point in time you started seeing some delay.
- Compare **the standard deviations** (see Chapter 3) of the delivery time. You can find out the difference in variance depending on factors such as people, region, and the time of the day.

This rough analysis can be done in minutes if you have data and Microsoft Excel, and you can find out where there may be a problem. If there may be a problem, you should form a strong hypothesis for a more detailed analysis. On the other hand, if you don't detect a problem, you should drop the priority of this hypothesis.

It's important to **not dig too deeply** while you are analyzing to form your hypothesis. Don't start a detailed analysis at this stage (e.g. decomposing data into different regions or time of day). You may end up losing the larger perspective and time to consider other hypotheses. As a result, you may overlook a more important hypothesis (and the analysis for that hypothesis).

Please refer to **Figure 0-4** regarding the analysis before building a hypothesis (first phase analysis), and the analysis after building a hypothesis to verify it (second phase analysis). In some cases, the problem may be too large or complex that you won't be able to (or won't need to) make a distinction between the two types of analysis.

Fig. 0-4 Two analysis phases for different purposes

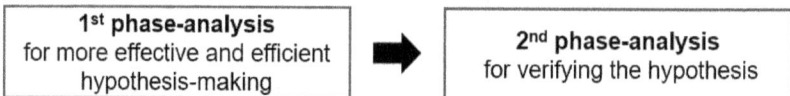

1st phase-analysis for more effective and efficient hypothesis-making	➡	2nd phase-analysis for verifying the hypothesis

Know the difference between a quick analysis to make a guess (first phase analysis) and a detailed analysis for logical reasoning (second phase analysis). You will succeed by choosing the right type of analysis at the right time.

Alex came up with the following objective, hypotheses and analysis methods.

Objective	To prove why it is important to enter the market in Country X
Hypotheses	Hypotheses which support the importance of entering this market:

1. Country X has market potential for cyclonic vacuum cleaners.
2. There are effective sales strategies.
3. The expected sales and expenditures in this business are reasonable.

Analysis Methods   To prove the hypotheses, Alex will analyze the following data:

- Data showing the number of people planning to purchase cyclonic vacuum cleaners
- Data showing which sales strategy is the most effective
- Data that predicts the sales and expenditures required in selling the products

Boss: "It's good that you're planning to prove whether the business is feasible by looking into sales and expenditures. If you explain the sales strategy in detail, it would strengthen your argument as well. Don't assume that 'Country X is the best target,' though, because having that bias would make you want to choose information that only supports that assumption."

Column: Using the Comprehensive Approach

In the section "Three Reasons Why You Need a Hypothesis," I explained **the comprehensive approach,** which is useful in the following situations.

For example, if it costs too much to obtain new data, and the data that you have is limited, then that data may not be very useful in setting the objective or verifying the hypothesis. Even in such a situation, you can try extracting as much information as possible from your data by using the comprehensive approach.

Let's look at a lesson learned from my experience.

We conducted an employee satisfaction survey consisting of a few dozen questions to obtain employee feedback regarding the workplace. However, we could not understand the reasons behind the feedback that we received. For example, we asked our employees "whether they were satisfied with their jobs". They gave us ratings on a scale of one to five, but we did not know the reasons behind their ratings or what kind of actions need to be taken to improve workplace satisfaction. We already used up our time and resources and could not conduct another survey, so we checked every single question and looked for any relation between the questions.

We found strong connections (correlations) between the ratings for "Are you satisfied with your job?" and "Did your accomplishment at work lead to career advancement?" and were able to think in detail how we could satisfy our employees.

Try using the comprehensive approach in cases like this, when you form a hypothesis but can't obtain any more data to verify your hypothesis.

Chapter 1

Effective Ways to Collect and Analyze Data

—When You Can't Find The Perfect Set of Data

Collecting Data at Random is No Good

Boss: "Good job, Alex! It looks like you set a goal and know what to do."

Alex: "Thanks. I feel exhausted from thinking...but it's clear what I need to do next."

Boss: "This is just the beginning! Tomorrow, please start collecting any data that you think may be necessary. We don't have much time. Keep in mind *what you're trying to say* with the data."

The next morning, Alex collected as much important looking data as possible within the company. At 11:00 a.m., the assignment was still unfinished.

Boss: "You look very busy. How is your data collection going?"

Alex: "I went to several departments. They all told me 'We don't have that kind of data.' I also searched online, but I only found basic information. I can't find exactly what I'm looking for."

Boss: "Are you just trying to find something that you can copy and paste? ...Yup. You won't find that kind of data anywhere unless you pay someone to do your job. We don't have that kind of time and budget. You'll have to get creative."

Alex: "Creative? What do you mean?"

Alex looked puzzled.

Boss: "You shouldn't expect to find any data that's ready to use. <u>Process your data so that it can be utilized more easily</u>. You don't need specialized knowledge or methods to do this. You just need a good idea."

Alex: "Would you please teach me?"

Boss: "Let's see what you've got, and think about how to reorganize it...but don't show me everything. You can't just randomly use whatever data you have. You need to consider how you're planning to use it."

Alex learned once again that preparing data is an extremely difficult task, but his boss gave him great advice.

Look for data that answers your hypothesis.

Ask yourself "What do I need to accomplish this?" and build a pyramid structure.

As you have seen in Alex's case, even if you know exactly what you need, there will be obstacles when you actually try to collect data. You would be very lucky if you found the relevant data within your company. In many cases, the data which you are searching for is only accessible to certain departments or people, and you may be unable to find and contact the right people to gain access to the data.

To verify your hypothesis, start by clarifying *what data you really need*. Otherwise, you may shift your focus to *how you can use the limited data that you already have*, which may distort your conclusion.

Ask yourself "What data do I need?" to verify the hypothesis. Let's use the "Objective→Hypothesis→Analysis Method" flow which was discussed in the Preface.

In Figure 1-1, I decomposed the hypothesis and dug one step deeper into the pyramid structure. By breaking things down to this level, you can clarify what you need to find out and what kind of data is necessary for that.

In an ideal situation, the factors at the bottom level of the pyramid structure would fulfill MECE (Mutually Exclusive, Collectively Exhaustive). Nevertheless, it is not your ultimate goal to strictly follow MECE. Just try your best.

Fig. 1-1 An example of the Pyramid structure

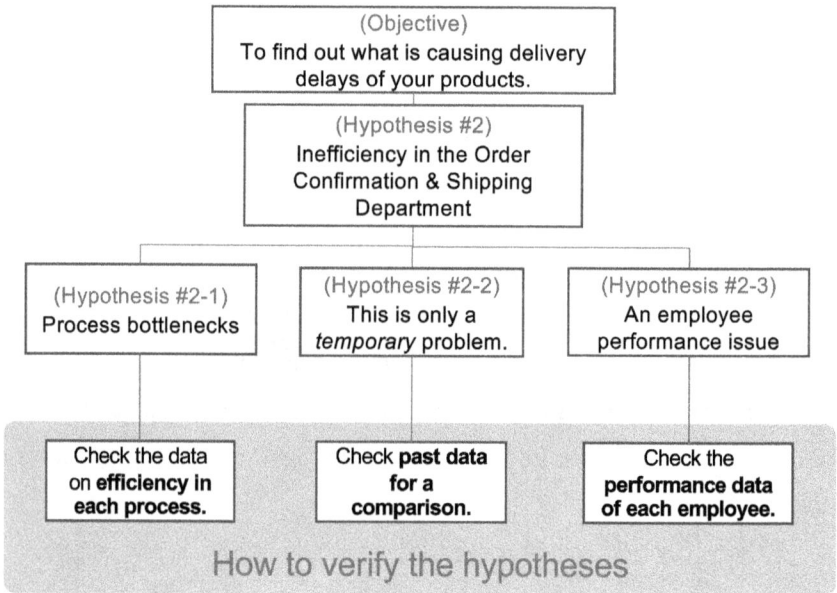

```
                    (Objective)
          To find out what is causing delivery
                delays of your products.

                  (Hypothesis #2)
              Inefficiency in the Order
              Confirmation & Shipping
                    Department

  (Hypothesis #2-1)    (Hypothesis #2-2)    (Hypothesis #2-3)
  Process bottlenecks  This is only a       An employee
                       temporary problem.   performance issue

  Check the data       Check past data      Check the
  on efficiency in     for a                performance data
  each process.        comparison.          of each employee.

              How to verify the hypotheses
```

Despite how important it is to decide which data should be used as input for your analysis, there is a large amount of choices of data. Furthermore, there is not a single right answer.

Say, you want to collect data to check whether a product is in demand and selling well. There are many ways to do this, and you may end up with different results depending on the focus—the point in time, sales region, or the type of customers to which it was sold.

> # Data Collection Tip No.1:
> # Collect enough data for your hypothesis and a little extra just in case.

What, then, do you need to know to collect data efficiently and as a good input for a higher quality analysis?

Analyze efficiently with a wider range of data collection.

In the "Objective→Hypothesis→Analysis Method" flow, getting from the Hypothesis to the Analysis Method is not easy. Even if you have a hypothesis, you may not reach your goal right away.

It is not always the case that you have a good hypothesis at the beginning and sufficient data to support it. In reality, the project may grow larger and more complicated as you proceed. You might go back and forth between the Hypothesis and Analysis Method stages to gradually reach your goal.

In such a case, you may not reach your conclusion if you limit your data collection to only that which is precisely necessary at that point for it to then be analyzed later.

Additionally, you may have done some analysis by then and it would be inefficient and exhausting to restart collecting any new data.

Instead, collect a little extra data at the beginning, even though it may be outside the scope of your hypothesis, to make things easier later on. Collecting data from a larger perspective can be helpful in the following cases.

1. Use your main data as a benchmark for other data.

Suppose you want an analysis on a certain product of your company. You need to collect data about the product to understand its characteristics, but you might also want to collect data on competitors' products so that you could compare the results of your analysis between your products and competitors'.

Say, you need a strategy to sell your products in Region A. You can collect and analyze data for Regions A, B and C to check whether Region A has distinctive characteristics compared to other regions. You would not have found this information if you had only collected data for Region A.

2.   Avoid running out of data.

Even if you may only need monthly data to verify your hypothesis, you might want to collect weekly and daily data to make things easier later on. For instance, even if you found out from your monthly data that sales had been dropping, up until April, when it started increasing again, you may not be able to detect the reason behind the change, as monthly data is too general for analyzing a retail business. If you had prepared weekly data, you might have found out that the increase in sales was due to a special promotion during the second week of April.

Although this does not mean that you should collect excess data all the time, please note that you would not know how helpful the data would have been for conducting a more profound analysis or producing a better outcome until later on. If you can easily obtain a little more data, go through this extra procedure.

You might waste some time and effort at first, but throughout your experience, you will gradually sharpen your intuition for what kinds of extra data may be useful.

> # Data Collection Tip No.2:
> # Focus on the attribute of your data.

Most statistical data used in business have **attributes** such as "time," "place," "product," "age," or "customer attributes." Collect data from these viewpoints and you will have a wider range of analysis.

Suppose you obtained monthly sales data. If you focus on the attribute of "time," you could also prepare weekly and daily data, increasing the types of data available. The weekly and daily data will give you different perspectives and analysis results compared to monthly data.

Using the same data, look from a different perspective by changing the attribute.

There may be several attributes in your data. Let's look at some examples:

Data: sales data for Product A

Attributes:
Time: sales data for the previous year, this month, or the previous Thursday
Place: sales data for Asia, the store in Pasadena, California, or the district covered by salesperson X
Customer: in their twenties, male or female, or whether that person purchased other items with the product

As you can see, collecting data with the idea that there are different attributes to account for could help you out if you get stuck while doing your analysis. It could also support your conclusion from different angles. *Utilize the same data in different ways* by focusing on different attributes.

Decompose and aggregate data by attributes.

If you focus on the attributes of your data, you can **decompose** and **aggregate** it.

"Time" is an example of an attribute. With data recorded over time (time-series data), you can change the units (annual, monthly, weekly) freely as long as you have the data. For example, if you currently have monthly data, you can decompose it into two parts (the first half and second half of the month), or into weekly or daily data.

You can do the same with "place." Data for each county can be aggregated into state or national data, or decomposed into cities, towns, or business districts, for example.

Please remember that you can decompose and aggregate data by considering its attributes.

Let's take a detailed look into what would happen if you decompose and aggregate data.

Figures 1-2 to 1-4 are three different graphs based on the same data. Notice how your results change dramatically depending on the unit in focus.

In **Figure 1-2**, there is a sharp plummet in the sales data in the second half of the month.

In the weekly data shown on **Figure 1-3**, figures are declining gradually, but there is also a risk of overlooking the fact that there were only three days in the fifth week which account for its sharp fall.

Figure 1-4 is a more detailed daily data graph. Even though there is a slump in the figures in the middle of the month, you can see the strong recovery toward the end of the month, which went undetected in Figures 1-2 and 1-3 due to aggregation.

Fig. 1-2 Half-month trend graph

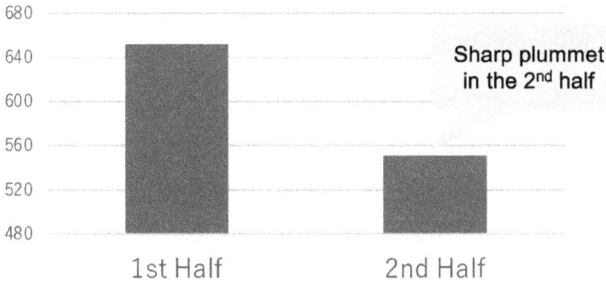

Sharp plummet
in the 2nd half

680
640
600
560
520
480

1st Half   2nd Half

Fig. 1-3 Weekly trend graph

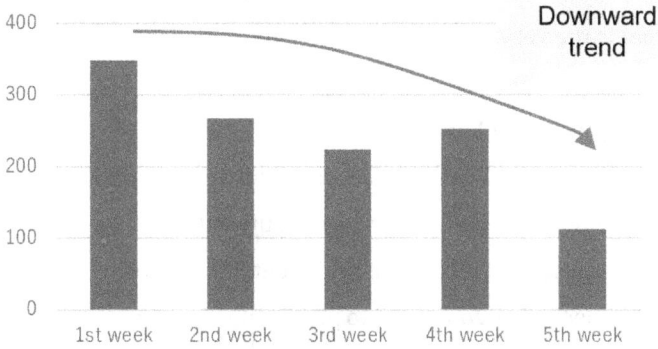

Downward
trend

400

300

200

100

0

1st week   2nd week   3rd week   4th week   5th week

Fig. 1-4 Daily trend graph

70
60
50
40
30
20
10
0

2021/9/1 2021/9/3 2021/9/5 2021/9/7 2021/9/9 2021/9/11 2021/9/13 2021/9/15 2021/9/17 2021/9/19 2021/9/21 2021/9/23 2021/9/25 2021/9/27 2021/9/29

Recovered at the
end of the month

The more you decompose the data, the more detailed your input information is going to be.

To what level should you decompose data?

Not everyone decomposes data down to the atomic level all of the time. Let's look at the following cases.

- **Case 1: Cost of Analysis**

    It is very rare that the data is already decomposed at the beginning. You will not know for sure (or find out visually) whether the results would change until you actually decompose the data in different levels.

    Thus, it is understandable that people tend to go straight into analysis, using the obtained data as it is without a second thought. Reorganizing data and redoing analysis, or paying attention to hidden issues is in itself very time and energy consuming. That is the very cost of analysis.

- **Case 2: An Increase in Variance**

    There also tends to be some irregular figures in a detailed set of data. For instance, in daily sales data, you may see a significant increase in sales on a day when there was a special promotion or sale event. Decomposing and having more detailed data than necessary could lead to picking up changes in data due to irregular factors. You may not be able to see the bigger picture when analyzing data with such variance.

    Therefore, you should not decompose all types of data without thinking. You need to determine to what level the data needs to be decomposed depending on how detailed your analysis should be based on your objective.

    In general, I like to decompose data one level further than the level that is necessary in reaching my ultimate objective.

Data Collection Tip No.3:
Think about the scope of data that suits your objective.

The level of decomposition is not the only factor affecting the result of your analysis. You also need to consider **the scope of data** to be used.

Say, you obtained the stock price data shown in **Figures 1-5 to 1-8**.

Figure 1-5 is based on the data for one day only. If someone were to ask about the current situation, you would look at this graph and answer that the stock price is <u>rising</u>.

Figure 1-6 is the graph for the week. Here, the stock price is also <u>rising</u>.

The monthly graph (**Figure 1-7**) looks different compared to the first two graphs. The figures rose at first, but you can see that that they are mostly dropping throughout the graph. If you were to be asked the same exact question, you would answer that the stock price is <u>dropping</u>.

There are too many fluctuations in the annual graph (**Figure 1-8**) to accurately explain its characteristics.

Thus, if you want to explain data from a set point in time, up until the present, your conclusion will change depending on the scope of the data which you are looking at. I am not just talking about the appearance of the graph. Having a different scope of data will provide a different set of information to be used as input in your analysis, as well as affect your analysis result.

There is no single correct way in determining the scope. You need to select the scope on a case-by-case basis in order to achieve an accurate result if you want to reach your objective.

You can avoid the risk of overlooking changes in your analysis results due to the selection of the scope of your data by analyzing data with different scopes and comparing them.

Fig. 1-5 Stock chart (1 DAY)

Fig. 1-6 Stock chart (1 WEEK)

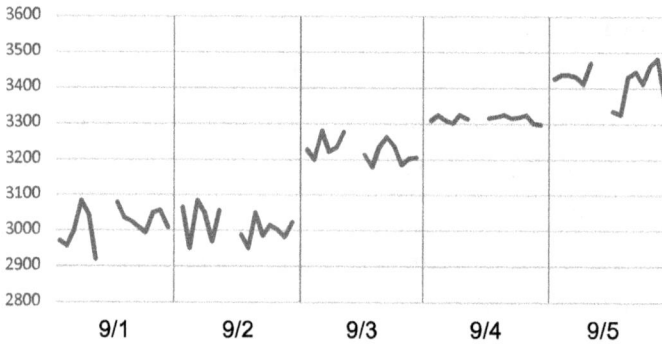

Fig. 1-7 Stock chart (1 MONTH)

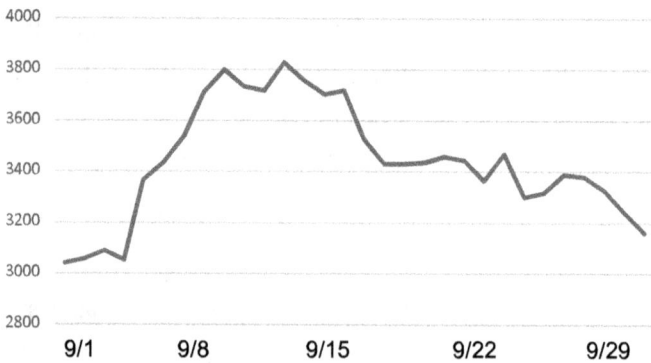

Fig. 1-8 Stock chart (1 YEAR)

Give a reasonable explanation about your scope.

So, then, how do you determine the scope of your data? This may not be as relevant in cases where the difference in scope is not of great importance in relation to your objective, or if you notice a similar trend recurring in a cycle.

In other cases, however, you will need to give a reasonable explanation about how you chose your scope as you present your data.

One way of doing this is to choose and analyze data with different scopes and show each of their results.

Example:

"The monthly data shows a trend that..., while the weekly data shows a trend that... This difference is due to ..."

This will provide a more profound analysis to your audience.

Please note that you will need to go one step further and evaluate the factors that led to any differences in your results instead of simply showing the results. Otherwise, having multiple conclusions could confuse your audience.

Data Collection Tip No.4:

Think of reasons to exclude outliers.

—*Why There Was a Big Change in the Sales Revenue of the Drugstore*

Outliers (Figure 1-9) are data points that have an outstanding value which are obviously very different from the rest of the data.

The characteristics of an outlier may affect the outcome of your analysis significantly, and you may not be able to reach the result you were looking for.

Suppose 50 customers purchased items at a drugstore during set hours of the day, and the average expenditure turned out to be $26.40.

If one of your customers spent $200.00, the average expenditure will rise to $30.40. There is a $4.00 difference per customer between the old data and the new data when you include the high-spending customer.

$26.40 (average expenditure) ×50 customers = $1,320.00 (total sales revenue)
$30.40 (average expenditure) ×50 customers = $1,520.00 (total sales revenue)

$1,520.00 - $1,320.00 = $200.00 (difference in total value)
$30.40 - $26.40 = $4.00 (difference in average value)

When your audience receives this information, they might think that there is a $4.00 difference in spending for every customer. The truth is, however, that only one customer spent a lot of money. Your result may mislead your audience to believe that the increase in the average expenditure is based on the behavior of all of the customers.

Fig. 1-9 Outlier

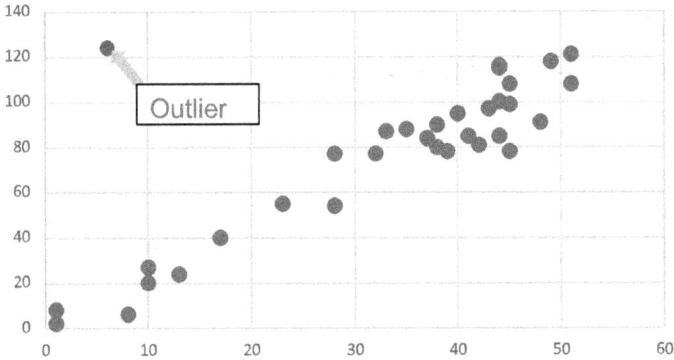

However, it is not always wrong to have an outlier.

More importantly, while you are analyzing data you need to remember that outliers exist. If there is an outlier without a valid reason, you should omit it before your analysis.

Draw scatter diagrams to find outliers.

Depending on the size of your data, you may miss any outliers if you only look at a list of raw data. To detect outliers efficiently, visualize your data using a graph such as a scatter diagram, and then determine the reason why the outlier is so different from the rest of the data.

Let's use the previous example of the drugstore. Say, you drew a graph and detected the outlier visually to identify the high-spending customer. Then, you found that she bought a $200 fitness equipment which is not very popular, and this equipment is only purchased every few years. In such a case, you may decide not to use this outlier for the purpose of calculating the average expenditure on general products.

If you keep repeating your analysis and your results don't look right, it is possible that an undetected outlier is affecting your results. You may not even notice the outlier until you reach that point. You need to be aware of the possibility of outliers in order to find them more easily.

On the other hand, please be careful not to omit outliers unconditionally or intentionally just to achieve a "better" result from your analysis (This is more tempting than we can imagine).

The Reality:
Adding Data Due to Insufficiency

The Obstacles We Face in Reality During Data Collection

In our day-to-day business, data collection is not as easy as it may seem. There may not be a problem when you have enough time and money, but in reality, we often end up with:

- data existing in your own department;
- data obtained from other departments in your company;
- data found on the internet; and
- any other data that you can find.

There is a disparity between *data that we need* derived theoretically from the pyramid structure (explained in the Preface and in this chapter) and *data that we can actually find*.

Is there a way to improve our analysis, even with this limitation? Yes, in this case, we can conduct **data processing**.

Process and create different types of data.

One way to obtain more information is to keep searching for data online, but you also have the option to utilize data that is already available to you.

Even if you are testing the same hypothesis, you can do so from different angles using the same data. Learn how to process your existing data in order to utilize it in many ways.

1.   Change the absolute value to a ratio.

In business, we mainly use two types of data: ratio and absolute value. When discussing sales revenue, for example, "$50,000 in May" is absolute value, and "$50,000 per month" is ratio data.

When collecting data, you will normally have a set of absolute values unless someone has already edited that data.

If absolute values are not helpful, try editing data into ratio and see if it helps.

Here is an example:

Figure 1-10 is the result of a survey regarding the number of subscriptions of smartphones in several cities. Data on men and women were collected separately. This type of data can be easily found online, through government websites, white papers, and other reports issued by research institutes.

It is difficult to discover any meaningful information from this kind of data (By "meaningful," I mean, being able to identify the characteristics of your data such as relatively more or less, or higher or lower, for instance.).

In Figure 1-10, the absolute values (numbers of subscriptions) will not tell you anything if the size or population of each city is different.

In order to understand the characteristics of your data, arrange the data onto a "level playing field" before comparing them; you should convert your data for each city into *per capita*.

Figure 1-11 is the result after processing the data.

Do you see the difference?

Fig. 1-10 The number of smartphone subscribers, 2010

(000 subscribers)	City A	City B	City C	City D
Male	18.3	24.1	78.8	45.3
Female	12.5	8.9	56.6	20.9
Total Population	221,000	374,000	629,000	566,000

Convert these numbers into penetration ratios

Fig. 1-11 The number of smartphone subscribers per capita (Penetration ratio) , 2010

(000 subscribers)	City A	City B	City C	City D
Male	0.08	0.06	0.13	0.08
Female	0.06	0.02	0.09	0.04

Calculations:

City A		City C	
Male	$18,300 \div 221,000 \fallingdotseq 0.08$	Male	$78,800 \div 629,000 \fallingdotseq 0.13$
Female	$12,500 \div 221,000 \fallingdotseq 0.06$	Female	$56,600 \div 629,000 \fallingdotseq 0.09$
City B		City D	
Male	$24,100 \div 374,000 \fallingdotseq 0.06$	Male	$45,300 \div 566,000 \fallingdotseq 0.08$
Female	$8,900 \div 374,000 \fallingdotseq 0.02$	Female	$20,900 \div 566,000 \fallingdotseq 0.04$

What you can tell after converting Figure 1-10 into Figure 1-11:

- Cities A and D have a similar penetration ratio and do not show a large difference in either men or women.

- City B has the lowest penetration ratio, while City C has the highest.

Converting numbers into the same base would not only make it easier to compare them, but would also allow for them to be used effectively as input data for various types of analysis. Comparing the data in Figures 1-10 and 1-11 for City

A, the numbers 18.3 (in thousands), or 18,300 male subscribers total, and 0.08 male subscribers per capita are very different. In other words, you now have an additional set of data derived from the original data.

If you want to convert absolute numbers into the same basic unit, you can divide the figures by the total. In Figure 1-10, the number of subscribers was divided by the population in each city. In other cases, you can convert absolute numbers into annual or monthly data, or per unit area or per length and the like.

As you can see in the chart below, units are not the only factors in converting data into ratio.

Category	Example
Ratio per unit	• Per capita
	• Per household
	• Per employee
	• Annual, monthly, weekly or daily
	• Per sale
	• Per X amount of dollars
	• Per unit area, etc.
Ratio by attribute	• Gender, age, etc.
Ratio by time	• Year-Over-Year (YOY), Average Annual Growth Rate (AAGR), etc.
Comparison with others	• Comparison with competitors, other countries, other industries, etc.

You can use the same exact data in various ways by processing it.

2.   Decompose data by factor to obtain more data.

As explained in "Data Collection Tip No.2," look from a different perspective by decomposition. If you decompose the data for each attribute (time, gender, region, etc.), you will have different sets of data for each attribute. You might even be able to glean new information which could not be found in the original data.

Here is an example.

Fig. 1-12 Relation between the No. of purchase and Age (TOTAL)

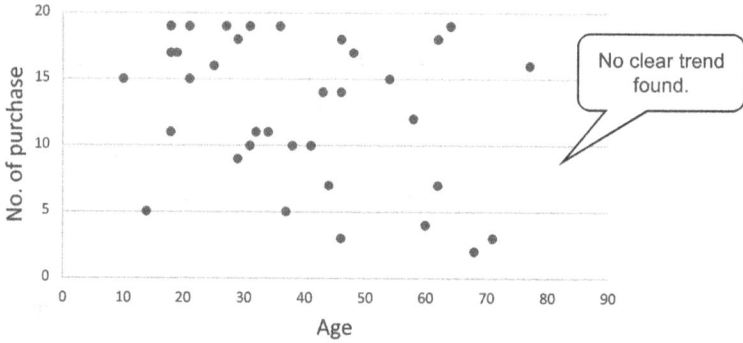

No clear trend found.

Fig. 1-13 Relation between the No. of purchase and Age (MALE)

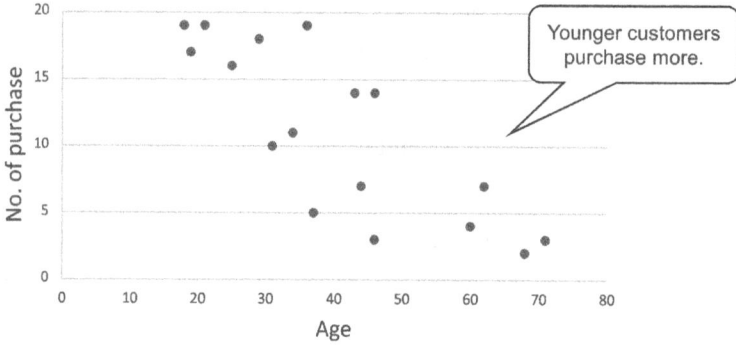

Younger customers purchase more.

Fig. 1-14 Relation between the No. of purchase and Age (FEMALE)

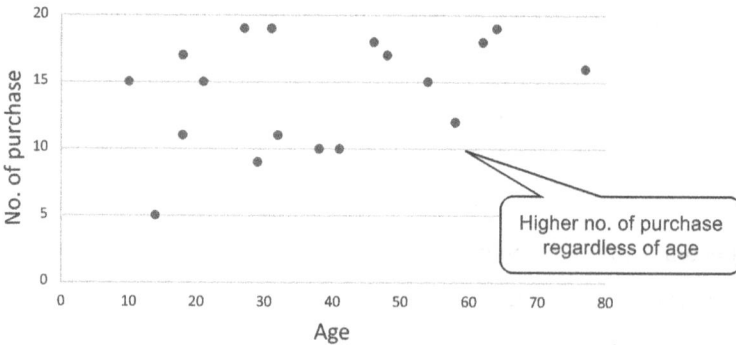

Higher no. of purchase regardless of age

Figure 1-12 shows the age of each customer and the number of products which they have purchased at a department store. Based on your expectation (hypothesis), you have drawn this graph to find a relation between customer age and number of items purchased, but you have learned nothing so far.

Don't give up just yet.

Customers have other attributes: occupation, home address and distance from home to the store, frequency of visiting the store, etc. Not all of these data points can be collected, but you could throw out your opportunity if you give up too early and do not explore the data any further.

Other than the age of customers, also consider whether gender may affect the sales data (It is important to come up with different ideas like these.).

If you can obtain such decomposed data, you can make two additional graphs as shown in **Figures 1-13** and **1-14**.

Excluding men aged sixty and older, you can see from the graph that young men tend to purchase more products, while the number of products purchased declines with age. There isn't a large difference in the behavior of women of different ages, but overall, they tend to buy more products compared to men.

You wouldn't have noticed these characteristics before decomposing the original data into those of men and women. This is how you may find additional information by decomposing data.

3. **Convert qualitative data into quantitative data to gather more information.**

The prerequisite for data analysis is that you have numerical data.

As I mentioned earlier in the chapter, if you have any data, you can process it to obtain different types of data.

However, you may get stuck if you can't find data that suits your objective (or if you have any budget limitations, etc.) in the first place. In such cases, try using this idea:

Instead of just collecting data, make your own data.

Why don't you use qualitative data from an existing survey taken by a number of people in the past (in the form of comments and descriptions in sentences), for instance?

Convert qualitative data into quantitative data by counting the number of times each keyword was mentioned in the comments, organizing the comments into several categories, and counting the comments in each category to calculate ratios. Such information can be used in your analysis. Positive and negative feedback can be counted separately to form data as well.

Remember, you need to read the information from the comments accurately and organize them into bullet points. Don't oversimplify by merging two different ideas into one. On the other hand, don't categorize too much so that there are only one or two data points in each category. The data wouldn't be sufficient input for your analysis.

Keep these points in mind as you convert your qualitative data into quantitative data.

To categorize information, you need to fully understand what the interviewed person was trying to say in the comments. Don't interpret their comments to mean something else just to suit your needs.

Don't be discouraged by obstacles. Think of different ways to create your own unique data. This is an important quality that every great analyst should have.

Alex checked the kind of information necessary for his business plan and looked for some data, but could not find data that was spot on in order to reach an answer.

Alex didn't give up. He knew that the group that sat next to him in his office had the sales data for cyclonic vacuum cleaners in Country Y. They had collected data on past sales revenue, prices and promotions.

Alex: "Although this is the data for Country Y and not X, I may be able to use this data by converting it from absolute value to ratio and decomposing it so that it can be used."

Boss: "The market is highly competitive and rapidly changing, so the price data from two years ago is too old. Just use the data from the last 12 months."

Alex: "You're right. I also followed your advice to gather extra data, so I obtained data for other countries besides X and Y. I'll look out for outliers and adjust the data before applying it to the analysis."

Boss: "Looks like you're getting the hang of things. When you're done, the next step will be analysis. Good luck!"

COLUMN: BEWARE OF ILLUSIONS FROM GRAPHS WITH RELATIVE DATA!

If you want to show the relative change in data from a certain point in time (starting point), be careful how you choose the scope of your data. For example, if you had a graph that showed the chronological change in sales data (**Figure 1-15**), you can make another graph (**Figure 1-16**) showing relative changes by focusing on a certain point in time (starting point: 100).

Fig. 1-15 Chronological Change in Sales Figures

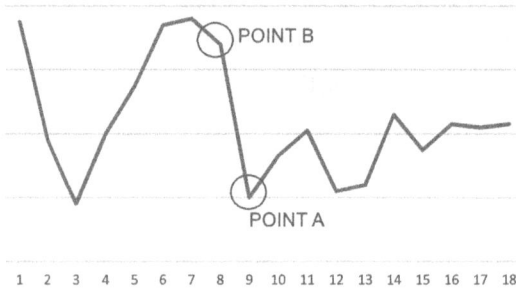

Fig. 1-16 Relative Trend From Point A

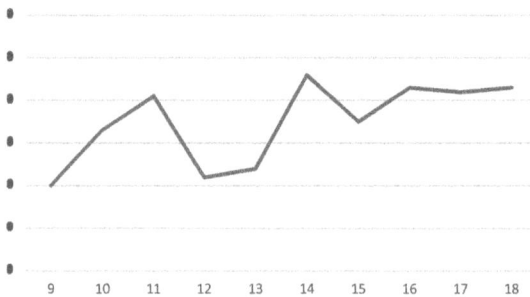

Figure 1-16 shows Point A as the starting point and has an upward trend. In sales, many people might associate this graph with market expansion.

On the other hand, when you shift your graph and show Point B as the starting point (**Figure 1-17**), the image is completely different. The new graph may give you the impression of a slump or stagnation.

Fig. 1-17 Relative trend from Point B

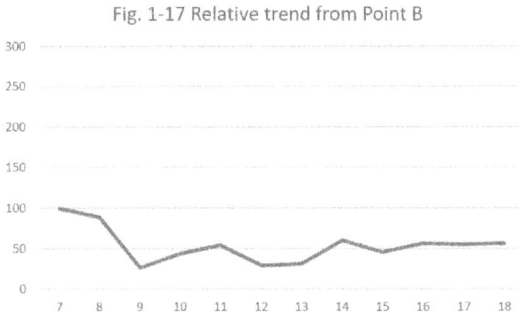

As you can see, when your graph shows relative values instead of absolute values, setting the right starting point is crucial.

Additionally, when you are an audience, don't be fooled when presenters select their scope of data arbitrarily.

Please be aware that these illusions may occur. At the very least, don't forget to ask yourself or the presenter why that particular scope of data (or starting point) was chosen.

Chapter 2

How to Estimate Profit

—Market Size, Average and Median

Assess the Size of the Market With a Bird's Eye View

Alex: "I finally collected enough data to get started with the analysis. I wouldn't have known who actually had useful data if I didn't ask the manager. It's good to have connections with the right people. Thank you for your advice."

Boss: "No problem. Data related to your job is often lying somewhere nearby within your own company. The problem is knowing how to find it. No one will organize internal data and bring it to you, so finding 'the right people' is key. Everyone is busy, so you need to work around this difficulty. "

Alex: "'People' are an important factor of data collection."

Boss: "Exactly. Anyway, let's focus on the current issue. We don't have much time left. Work on the analysis and create a business plan. Start working from a larger perspective such as market size and profitability. Finish it off with detailed strategies. We don't want to start off with strategies which don't support our prerequisites."

Alex: "What do you mean by 'starting with a larger perspective'?"

Boss: "We're entering a completely different market. What do you need to think of first? What is the largest perspective?"

Alex thought for a while and said:

Alex: "Largest perspective...Is that the market itself?"

Boss: "Exactly! You need to convince the audience that the market has potential. How to sell is not as paramount as market potential."

Alex: "That's true."

Boss: "When you're looking at something as large as the market, it's counterproductive to go too deeply into the details of what is happening inside of it. For example, checking the difference between the prices of products would not have a large impact on the whole market. You need a bird's eye view."

Alex: "I see, would you teach me how to do that?"

Boss: "I'll give you a hint: average."

Alex was surprised. Even elementary school kids knew what an average was. Although he was a little skeptical, he was willing to learn.

> ## Use the average to determine a representative value.
> *—What is the size of the market?*

Alex decided to "assess the size of the market" but wasn't sure how to obtain and use data to achieve that goal.

Data such as total sales revenue and the total number of potential customers are often used as indicators to describe "market size." The scope of the market could be defined by the "size of the entire market" including other companies, but it could also be limited to only the part of the market which is relevant for the sales of your products.

To make a business plan, you need to be able to see how much potential there is in the market for the sales of your products in Country X. This chapter will focus on this topic.

You need to clarify the definitions of key terms such as "market size" because the data required for an analysis depends on them. You must also share a common understanding with the audience before making a proposal (Don't assume that they understand what you mean). After organizing data and graphs for your presentation, don't just stop there. Write down the definitions in full detail to the point where you might even find it a little too meticulous.

Summarize a set of various numbers with the average.

What type of data is necessary to estimate the total sales revenue in a new market, then?

The market consists of an accumulation of sales of different products. Even when you limit the sales data to those of products sold by the same company, they could vary depending on the brand or grade of the products. Theoretically, if you add up all the sales, you may eventually reach the size of the whole market, but doing this is unrealistic.

It is inefficient, and you can't specify the price of each individual product to be sold in the future. Instead of looking at individual sales, go bold and use just one number to represent all data.

You can do this by calculating the average value of individual prices to be used as a representative price.

Simplify your concept of market size to "the average price multiplied by the number of products to be sold."

Market Size (Dollars) = Average Price (Dollars per Product)×Number of Products

So, how do you determine the "average price?"

If we are talking about a new product which is not in the market yet, you can simply use "the price at which the seller is willing to sell it" ("list price", etc.). You can also research the pricing of competitors and calculate the average, as you are likely to face competition once you enter the market.

If your company has experience selling a product in another market, using that data as a benchmark may provide an even more accurate and realistic analysis. If that product is the same as the one you are introducing in a new market, it would be great, as that data would be easy to find. Alex was able to find past sales data for Country Y (**Figure 2-1**). Country Y has very similar market characteristics as Country X such as culture, price of commodities, and manufacturing cost.

Fig. 2-1 Sales price results of cyclonic vacuum cleaners in Country Y (US$)

322	453	314	301	360	320	379	318	362	331	458	327	409
404	355	367	316	465	336	341	339	322	306	462	419	338
310	339	302	342	474	404	417	304	388	347	471	369	313
460	400	342	346	344	435	315	384	373	430	411	338	316
320	409	399	427	443	383	409	449	315	333	379	442	332
322	355	453	379	315	312	323	437	445	468	455	420	452
366	472	370	409	408	450	411	342	301	334	423	437	455
372	306	363	473	447	424	472	441	369	306	365	407	448
439	453	379	340	308	397	439	415	356	470	456	362	358
449	360	345	401	305	335	455	420	462	334	325	421	361
383	451	311	372	358	447	365	432	334	393	369	367	440
420	333	405	303	453	342	401	425	450	313	341	329	470
415	361	307	356	353	362	471	319	429	472	455	329	383

AVERAGE
US$368

It is unlikely for him to discover any meaning from this list of numbers, but by calculating the average, he can summarize the data set with one value which shows approximately "how big" the data set is overall, no matter how many numbers are in the data set.

Additionally, he can fix the average as a representative value and multiply it by variables to show the approximate total of the whole data set.

By using the data set shown in Figure 2-1, Alex calculated the average price in Country Y. It turned out to be $368.

In **Figure 2-2,** the pricing of 30 products were randomly chosen to create a bar graph. You can calculate the total price for all products by adding (the area of) each bar. (In this example, add all 30 values, $322+404+... and the total is approximately $11,045.)

You can simplify this task. Estimate the total by multiplying the average value by the size of data. In this case, the average is $368. Multiply that by 30, and your total is $11,040. That is the area of the rectangle shown in **Figure 2-3**.

Comparing the two figures, you can see how much easier it is to use the average value as a way of calculation (and as a way of thinking).

Fig. 2-2 Total revenue from the 30 sample data

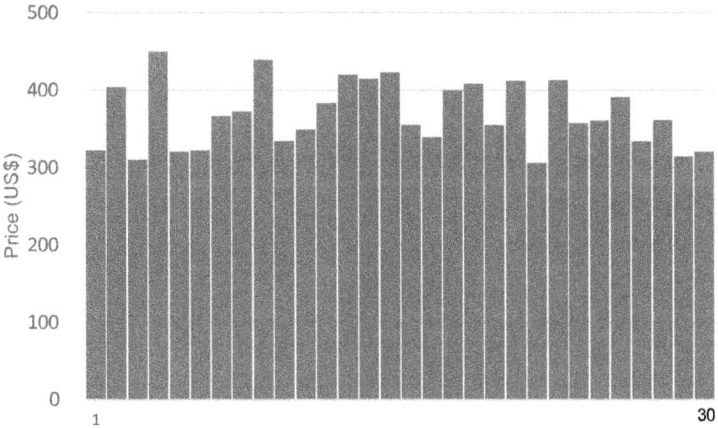

Fig. 2-3 Total sales revenue (Average price x the No. of sales)

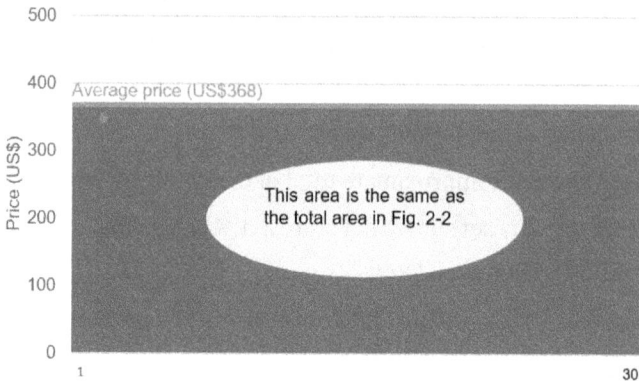

Use the average to deal with unforeseeable factors.

When you're in the planning stage of a business, there are uncertain factors such as the sales forecast. In the previous example, you can't conclude the number of products to be sold. It might be 30, 50, or 100.

In that case, instead of fixing the number of products, fix the price (use the average value) and keep the number of products as a variable. You can simply multiply the average price by the number of products to calculate the total amount in any situation, whether the number of products is 30, 50, or 100. In **Figure 2-4**, whether the width of the rectangle is long or short, you can still easily calculate the area by using the average.

This is an efficient and flexible method to make a rough estimate on the total value (in this case, the market size).

Fig. 2-4 Total sales revenue (by the No. of sales)

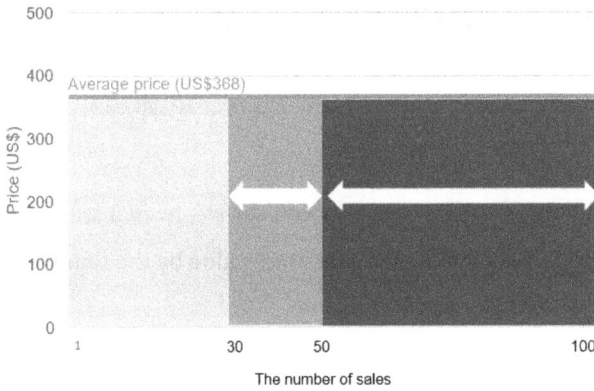

Estimate the number of products to be sold.

Next, how do we estimate the number of products to be sold?

This value cannot be controlled by the seller, and you can't simply calculate the average value of the sum as I explained in Figure 2-1 (average price for X amount of products). Rather, you need to find a different approach depending on the characteristics of the market or product. We already know where the products will be sold, so there will be more accuracy. As it is often said in marketing, use segmentation (stratification) of potential customers. How large is the customer segment in that country? Within that segment, what percent of the market share can your company hold?

I will not go any further as this is not the main subject of this book, but you can use the sales data of other companies, your own company, or figures in other markets as a benchmark.

Conversely, you can also calculate the average number of products from the sales data of your competitor, and check the difference in total sales revenue when you change the price. In such cases, you need to determine the prerequisites of the business, restrictions, and which variable is going to be the strategic driver (the key factor that will affect your business) case-by-case.

The most important point is to not use several values as variables. Fix one value as a constant to make things easier to understand.

Does the average really represent all data?
—The Pitfalls of Relying on the Average

Let's review what we know about average, from a standard point of view. The average is calculated by dividing the total value by the number of values. What does this really mean? You might imagine:

- The value in the center
- The value which represents the whole data set
- The value which appears most frequently in the whole data set

These statements are not necessarily true, even though they sound plausible.

As we have seen in **Figures 2-2 and 2-3**, the average is the value reached when a set of different values (data) is "flattened." When you flatten the differences, it may seem like the average would fall right into the center, and a lot of data points would be scattered near the average, but that's not always true. Do you know why?

If a lot of numbers are scattered near the average value, the image would look like the bell curve in **Figure 2-5**. However, some types of data don't follow a normal distribution pattern (**Figures 2-6 and 2-7**).

In **Figure 2-6**, there is no data at or near the average value, and the actual data points are a lot more or a lot less than the average.

In **Figure 2-7**, there is a lot of data around the average value, but the average value is to the left of the majority of the data points.

Fig. 2-5 A typical assumption of "AVERAGE"

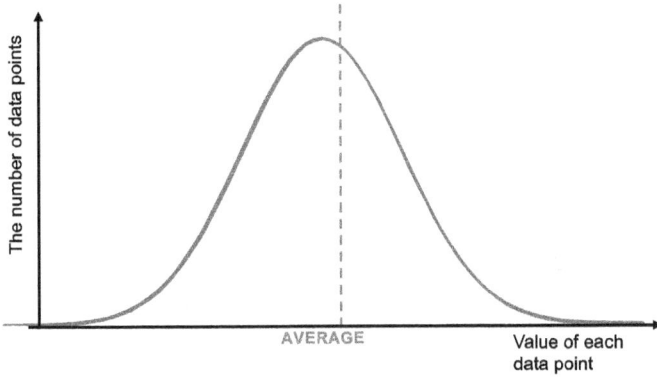

Fig. 2-6 Another type of "AVERAGE"

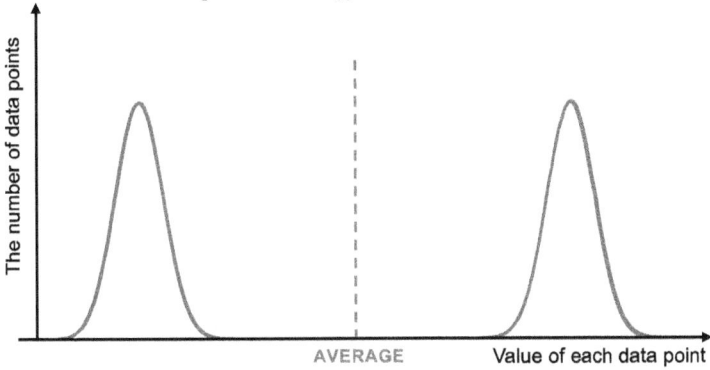

Fig. 2-7 Another type of "AVERAGE"

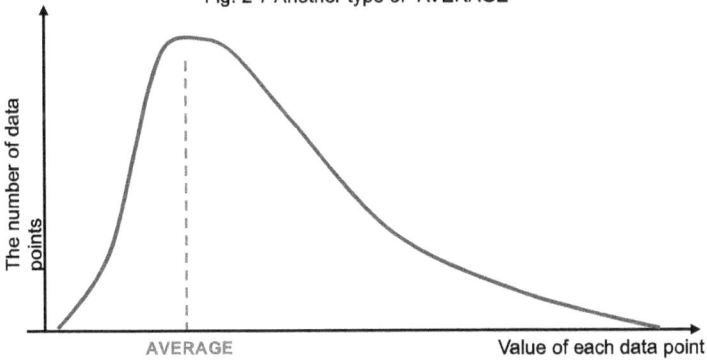

As you can see, <u>the average value is only the outcome of the total value</u>

divided by the number of values, and it has nothing to do with the data distribution (how data is scattered). Therefore, the assumption that the average is the center value, the value that represents the whole data set, or the most common value, is not always true.

However, many people are still under this mistaken impression.

This is what you should keep in mind:

1. **The average is not always at the center.**
2. **There isn't necessarily a large amount of data scattered near the average.**

The average can be calculated easily with a calculator. In business, however, you will often encounter a large set of data and will not have time to punch every number into the calculator. Use the "AVERAGE function" in Microsoft Excel. Select the cell range by typing it into the parentheses after the word "AVERAGE." The average value will then be shown. I recommend this shortcut if you need to save time.

Fig. 2-8 "AVERAGE" function in Excel

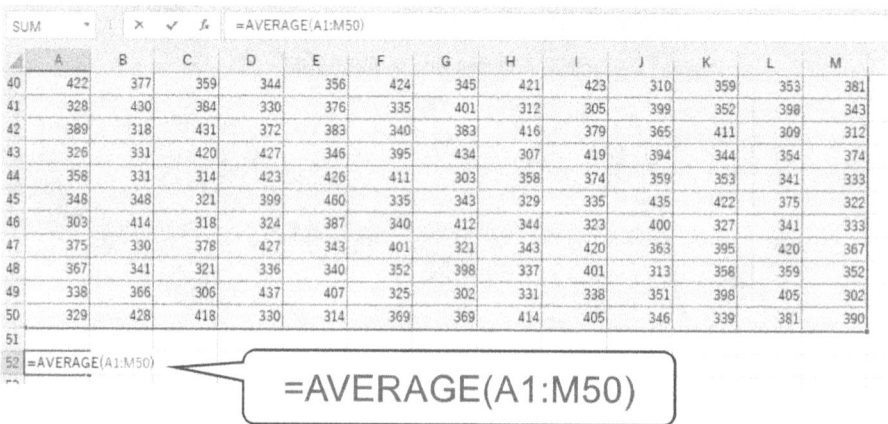

	A	B	C	D	E	F	G	H	I	J	K	L	M
40	422	377	359	344	356	424	345	421	423	310	359	353	381
41	328	430	384	330	376	335	401	312	305	399	352	398	343
42	389	318	431	372	383	340	383	416	379	365	411	309	312
43	326	331	420	427	346	395	434	307	419	394	344	354	374
44	358	331	314	423	426	411	303	358	374	359	353	341	333
45	348	348	321	399	460	335	343	329	335	435	422	375	322
46	303	414	318	324	387	340	412	344	323	400	327	341	333
47	375	330	378	427	343	401	321	343	420	363	395	420	367
48	367	341	321	336	340	352	398	337	401	313	358	359	352
49	338	366	306	437	407	325	302	331	338	351	398	405	302
50	329	428	418	330	314	369	369	414	405	346	339	381	390
51													
52	=AVERAGE(A1:M50)												

SUM   =AVERAGE(A1:M50)

=AVERAGE(A1:M50)

The median gives you a hint on the positioning of data.

How, then, can we solve the issues of using the average?

The solution to Issue No. 1 (the average is not always at the center) is the **median.**

The median is the middle value in the list of numbers, positioned right in the middle when you arrange data in the order of size.

If you have an odd number of values from least to greatest such as the five values 1, 6, 10, 15, and 28, the middle value **"10"** is the median of this data set.

If you have an even number of values in your data set such as the four values 1, 6, 10, and 15, **"8"**, the average value of the two middle values 6 and 10, is your median.

Here are the characteristics and advantages of using the median.

- **Prevent outliers from affecting the rest of your data.**

Outliers which are a lot larger than the rest of the data may affect your average significantly. You don't need to worry about this when you use the median. Since the median is exactly in the middle of the smallest and largest value, it will not be affected by outliers that are a lot larger or smaller. Even when using the same data, it will look very different to the audience depending on whether you present the average or median value.

- **The amount of data larger than the median is the same as the amount of data that is smaller.**

The *value* of each data determines the average, whereas the *amount* of data determines the median. As the median will be placed at the center of a set of data that has been arranged by size, there will always be an identical amount of data that is larger and smaller than the median.

This means that the median is an indicator showing the positions of each value in the set of data. For instance, if you compare your company with a list of competitors and you want to know whether your company is ranked higher or lower than the middle, the average will not tell you anything (It is amazing how many people have this misconception!), but the median will.

While this is slightly off topic, we tend to feel insecure or relieved when we know how we are doing compared to "the middle". You know by now that you may make a bad decision if you compare yourself with the average to see if you're doing well or not. For example, scoring above the average score on a test doesn't necessarily mean that you are in the top half of the class.

Let's use Figure 2-1 again, this time to calculate the median price of products sold in Country Y.

Use the "MEDIAN function" in Microsoft Excel. Select the cell range by typing it into the parentheses after the word "MEDIAN." The median value will then be shown (See **Figure 2-9**).

Fig. 2-9 "MEDIAN" function in Excel

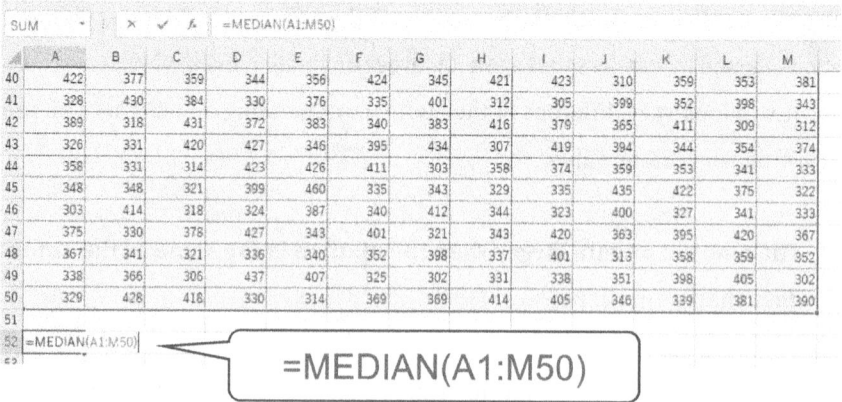

SUM		× ✓ ƒx	=MEDIAN(A1:M50)									
A	B	C	D	E	F	G	H	I	J	K	L	M
422	377	359	344	356	424	345	421	423	310	359	353	381
328	430	384	330	376	335	401	312	305	399	352	398	343
389	318	431	372	383	340	383	416	379	365	411	309	312
326	331	420	427	346	395	434	307	419	394	344	354	374
358	331	314	423	426	411	303	358	374	359	353	341	333
348	348	321	399	460	335	343	329	335	435	422	375	322
303	414	318	324	387	340	412	344	323	400	327	341	333
375	330	378	427	343	401	321	343	420	363	395	420	367
367	341	321	336	340	352	398	337	401	313	358	359	352
338	366	306	437	407	325	302	331	338	351	398	405	302
329	428	418	330	314	369	369	414	405	346	339	381	390

=MEDIAN(A1:M50)

=MEDIAN(A1:M50)

Compare the average and median to remove outliers.

Looking at the results, the median is $363, and the average is $368. The difference is very small. In this case, we can use either the median or the average to understand the big picture.

When there's a large difference between the average and the median, some data points may be very distinctive from the rest of the data. These are the earlier mentioned "outliers." A small number of outliers is pulling the average and causing the disparity between the average and the median.

In such a case, you need to identify any outliers and decide whether it's reasonable to include them in your data. If you're not sure, using the median may be helpful.

Therefore, you can compare the median to the average to filter out outliers.

The solution to Issue No. 2 (there is not necessarily a large amount of data scattered near the average) is using a histogram, which I'll explain in the next chapter.

> ## Use the average to make your first business decision before creating a plan.
> —*How many vacuum cleaners need to be sold to reach your goal?*

First of all, it is crucial to grasp the market size in order to assess the market potential for your business before getting into a more detailed analysis. It would be too late if, after giving a detailed analysis, you learned that you won't get a return on your investment within your prescribed period of time. You may also find out later that you could have entered a different market with more potential.

Make this initial judgement by using the easiest method in the world — the average.

Because this is just initial decision-making and not a final decision, this bold, efficient and simple method is really helpful. Don't just calculate the average without having an objective, though. Once you set your objective, using the average value is an effective strategy.

What is Alex's conclusion after calculating the average in sales for Country Y?

The difference between the average ($368) and the median ($363) is very small, so he decided to use the average value as a benchmark for entering the new market in Country X.

Suppose the population of Country X a year later is 20 million people, and the percentage of the middle and upper class who can purchase products in this price range is around 20%. You can easily obtain this type of general data online from a public institution. Demographics and other data can be found on government websites. The World Bank also provides statistics such as the World Development Indicators.

Say, you made observations on the competitors existing in the market of

Country X as well as the competitors that might enter the market in the future, and estimated that your company share might be about 2% (regarding these consumers in the middle and upper class).

Your estimate of the number of vacuum cleaners to be sold is:
20,000,000×20%×2% = 80,000 units

Multiply that by the average ($368).
$368×80,000 = $29,440,000

That is the estimated sales revenue. (In reality, you might also consider the growth rate of the market, politics, culture, and country risk, etc. but these factors will not be discussed in this book.)

The data of one city may change the national average...

Here is some practical advice.

Organizing data by nation is an easy way to look at the scope of the market. However, depending on the size and diversity of the nation, there's a risk of interpreting data inaccurately by lumping every region of the nation into one simple statistic of national data. Again, the average value may create an issue. The expenditure per capita in China and the expenditure per capita in Shanghai are very different. In other words, the data of a city may affect the national data. If you only look at the national average, you won't see the characteristics of the data of that city. When there's a large disparity between the data of a city (or region) and the national data, you should examine both data sets.

Determine how long it would take for the return on your initial investment.

You also need to be practical and think of profit as well as sales. For an average sales of $368, suppose your estimated profit was 15% bearing in mind the profit from past sales. The average profit per vacuum cleaner is: $368×15% = $55.20. Multiply the number of vacuum cleaners to be sold (80,000), as we did in calculating sales, and you would get $4.4 Million as the estimated total profit for the first year. If you suppose that the sales and profit would be around the same amount in subsequent years as well, you can determine how many years it would take to recover the return on initial investment (launching new stores, product development, cost of labor, etc.). This is extremely valuable information for decision making in management.

If the initial investment necessary is $18 Million, it would take about 4 years to recover this investment (18÷4.4 ≒ 4.1). (Note: There is a more detailed investment recovery theory, but I have simplified the calculation here.)

In general, when you are creating a business plan, you need to compare the minimum profit (ratio) necessary, goal or sales quota, and estimated profit, and verify its effectiveness.

If you use the average sales as the unit price, you can calculate backwards to find out how many vacuum cleaners need to be sold to reach the quota.

Suppose that your expected profit was $5.2 Million. Average profit per sale is $55.20.

$5,200,000÷$55.20≒94,000 units

Thus, approximately 94,000 units need to be sold to reach the expected profit.

As you can see, if you need to paint a big picture (e.g. market size), you can calculate the amount per unit (e.g. unit price) times quantity. In many cases, you can simply use the average value to get a rough idea.

Although using the average is convenient for summarizing a large amount of data with one value, there are some things to watch out for.

Keep in mind that the median value is a useful tool to check whether the average value is affected by numbers that are outstanding from the rest of the data (or to avoid this from happening).

As average values tend to be calculated easily without any thought, I recommend that you use both average and median values at all times.

Even though everyone in the company has been saying that "Country X has potential as a new market," Alex realized that he shouldn't assume that this was true. He had to check whether all the conditions were met in entering this market.

He also noticed that more than 90,000 vacuum cleaners needed to be sold to reach the expected profit.

Alex: "I didn't know that you could use the average value in these ways. Now I have a rough idea of the market size. I'll report to my boss tomorrow."

COLUMN: THINGS TO WATCH OUT FOR WHEN USING PUBLISHED DATA

I already discussed how to utilize the limited data that is available. You can also use published data which generally can be broken down into the following categories.

Data published by public institutions

This type of data is mostly available free of charge. The data is reliable, but often too generalized and not specialized in certain products, brands, or companies.

Data on a particular industry or product published or provided by individuals or consulting firms, etc.

This type of data is more practical because it specializes in particular fields of business. The reliability of data varies widely, however, and there's a risk from using it without checking the reliability (e.g. the original source of data or the conditions for the calculations are unclear, etc.).

In real life, you'll often need to consider information directly related to your company such as the industry, product, or market. In most cases, you won't find public data which is ready to be used to achieve a result aligned with your objective. For example, if you want to know "the market size for cyclonic vacuum cleaners for each country," it is impossible to find the exact data. Even if you find it, online data may not always be reliable.

I usually reach my answer by using only internal data, or by using a combination of internal and public data.

If you want to find out the age group and gender of your core customers, you can look for information existing within your company on other markets. However, if you need general information such as the population of a specific age group in a certain country, it's reasonable to look for the latest published data. Use these two different types of information to find out the size of the market that you're trying to penetrate.

Chapter 3

How to Estimate Risk

—Standard Deviation and Histograms

Identify risks. Things don't always go according to plan.

Alex: "I calculated the average to grasp the approximate size of the market in Country X and learned that entering this market is actually a lot more challenging than we had assumed, but selling 90,000 vacuum cleaners is not impossible."

Boss: "It's possible, but it won't be easy. First of all, do you really think 90,000 units is a sufficient amount to achieve our goal?"

Alex: "Why do you ask? It should be correct...I double-checked my calculation..."

Alex was baffled once again.

Boss: "I know, but I'm asking if that's a realistic number. You could propose to the board that our plan is to sell 90,000 units, and the budget is fine, but the board might ask you if the numbers are reliable. What will you say, then? There is no guarantee that our distributors would sell them at our list price."

Alex "True..."

Boss: "Business cannot rely on willpower or 'never say die' spirit. Doing your best is not enough... You need to understand the risks in your plan before making important business decisions."

Alex: "You're right. Not everything may go according to the plan. After all, I only calculated the average. I'm feeling anxious."

Boss: "The average is useful in summarizing a large set of data with one value, but there's a blind spot. You're ignoring the original set of data which had various numbers. This 'variance' of data may create a risk in your analysis results."

Alex: "The sales data for Country Y had various numbers too. Not all products were sold at the same price. If they were all sold at a discounted price, we would need to sell more than 90,000 units."

Boss: "It is not enough to conclude that 'there is a risk in the plan.' You have to specify the kind and the size of risk to make a decision. **Visualize it.**"

Alex: "OK, but how?"

Boss: "Here's a hint: **standard deviation**."

Alex: "Do you mean the standard deviation that we learn in school?"

Boss: "Yes. Here, let me show you."

Identifying Risks From Standard Deviation

Be ready to answer the question: "Is your plan really going to work?"

Things rarely go according to plan in business, or in life in general. Always keep this in mind when making a business plan. No matter how meticulously calculated and seemingly perfect your plan is, things may not go as expected (This is why Alex was warned by his boss).

In Chapter 2, I used the average to make a rough estimate of the size of the whole data set. Instead of looking at every single data point, the average summarizes the whole data set efficiently.

However, by focusing on the average, you are also ignoring the difference in the size of each value (data point) in the data set.

Variance shows how each of these points of data are distributed. As shown in Figures 2-5 to 2-7, even if the average value is the same, the actual data set may have different variance.

If Alex ignores the possibility that the products may be sold at a price which is lower than the expected average price, the business plan would only be "a pie in the sky" with hidden risks.

To answer the question whether "things would really go as expected," Alex needs to know what the risks are, where they lie (in sales, for example), and how they would affect the analysis results.

Thus, the degree of variance needs to be visualized.

Use standard deviation to show variance with numbers.

Standard deviation is a statistical method that shows the variance of each value (data point) when you have multiple values in your data set.

A large variance means that your data set has a wide range of numbers that are small and large.

Figure 3-1 shows a visual image of variance.

In this graph, you can see how far each value is from the average. The difference between each value and the average is called **"deviation."**

Deviation = Each Value – Average Value

Variance is an indicator that shows how scattered the numbers are as a whole, and is calculated by adding the square of Deviation for each value and then dividing it by the total number of values (data points).

Why do we need to square the number?

A data set has numbers that are smaller and larger than the average. If you simply add Deviation for each value and divide it by the total number of values, this will not be equal to the sum of the distance between the numbers and the average because there are both positive and negative deviations. For example, if the average value is 4, the sum of deviation for the data set (6 and 2) is 0, so you cannot use this equation.

$$(6 - 4) + (2 - 4) = 2 - 2 = 0$$

Therefore, you need to square the numbers.

However, squared values are hard to use, which is why you need to calculate the square root ($\sqrt{\ }$). By eliminating the effect of negative values and extracting the sum of the distance between each value (data point) from the average, you can show how scattered the data set is as a whole.

Here are the equations:

Deviation = Each Value – Average Value
Variance =the Sum of (Deviation) 2 / the Total Number of Data Points

Normal Distribution: Symmetrical on Both Sides

In Figures 3-1 and 3-2, a lot of values are near the average, and the total number of values (data points) decreases as your eyes shift away from the average. This is called **normal distribution** (It is commonly used to explain standard deviation). This data is perfectly symmetrical on both sides with a beautiful bell-shaped curve. This is an ideal image for understanding standard deviation.

A data variance which is close to normal distribution means that about two thirds of all data fit within the distance of standard deviation from the average, in both the positive and negative directions. If the standard deviation is 15, about two thirds of all data fit within the distance ±15 from average.

Fig. 3-1 An assumption of "variance"

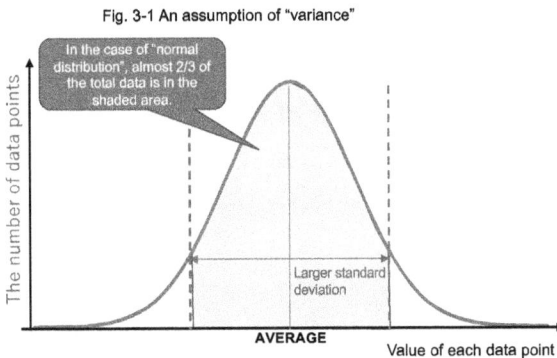

In the case of "normal distribution", almost 2/3 of the total data is in the shaded area.

The number of data points

Larger standard deviation

AVERAGE

Value of each data point

Fig. 3-2 Another assumption of "variance"

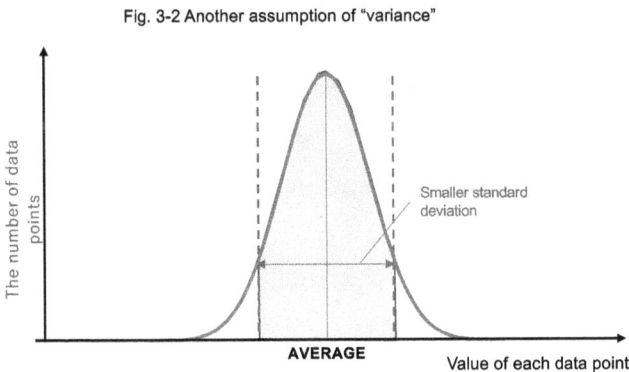

The number of data points

Smaller standard deviation

AVERAGE

Value of each data point

A small variance means that a lot of numbers in your data set are plotted close to a certain value (See **Figure 3-2**). In Figures 3-1 and 3-2, about two thirds of the data lie in the shaded area. This range is smaller in Figure 3-2, and the standard deviation is also smaller.

Here is a more detailed example.

Say, you counted the number of customers that came to a small store in one month. The average number of customers was 34.5 per day, and the standard deviation was 14.6 (**Figure 3-3**).

As I mentioned, if this data is deemed as normal distribution, about two thirds of all data should lie within 34.5±14.6. Therefore, you can use the standard deviation value to find out the range in which two thirds of all data fit in.

34.5 + 14.6 = 49.1
34.5 - 14.6 = 19.9

This means that two thirds of all data lie between the numbers 19.9 to 49.1. If we assume normal distribution, the number of customers who came to the store in about 20 days (out of 30 days total) was between 19.9 and 49.1 people per day.

Fig. 3-3 The standard deviation describes the range of the number of customers who came to the shop.

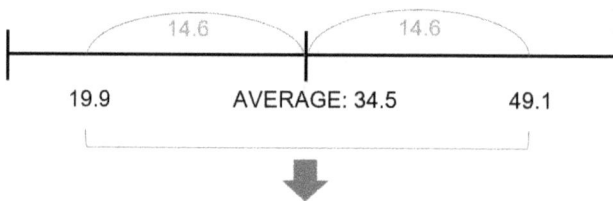

Almost 2/3 of all data lie within the range between 19.9 and 49.1. (19.9~49.1 customers visited the shop in almost 20 days out of a total of 30 days.)

Standard deviation shows the stability of your business.

So, in which situations in business (and how) can we use standard deviation?

Fig. 3-4 Business Stability, Risk and Standard Deviation

[AVERAGE]

1st Half	2nd Half
$50 Mil.	$50 Mil.

The sales revenue is the same.

[STANDARD DEVIATION (Weekly)]

1st Half	2nd Half
$20 Mil.	$10 Mil.

There is less weekly variance in the second half.

Weekly sales is more stable.

The best characteristic of standard deviation is that you can get a rough idea of the degree of variance of data, which cannot be achieved with the average. It helps you think like this: "This data has a very large variance, so it is not safe to rely only on the average value," or "Compared to the first half of the year, the average sales at this store is still the same in the second half of the year, but there is less weekly variance and sales is more stable." (See **Figure 3-4**)

Suppose the average monthly sales for one store were $50,000. That sounds like a lot, and a very stable amount, but what if the standard deviation were $35,000? That means that there is a large data variance within the range $50,000±$35,000.

Comparing the average ($50,000) and standard deviation ($35,000), I think that this is very risky business. Is it really safe to use the number $50,000 to represent the sales revenue of this store? On the other hand, business might be more stable if the standard deviation were only $3,000, and it should be fine to use the average $50,000. (The numbers $35,000 and $3,000 cannot be assessed precisely, so this is just based on my instincts.)

Calculate standard deviation using Excel (the STDEV function).

Although a slightly complicated equation including the square root is used to calculate standard deviation, you do not need to calculate this on your own. In most cases, the STDEV function in Microsoft Excel can be used to reach the answer immediately. Use the direct function in Excel, or follow these simple procedures:

STEP 1: Choose a blank cell and type "=STDEV ( )".

STEP 2: Left-click and select the data range, which will be displayed in the ( ) part of the function.

STEP 3: Press the ENTER key, and the standard deviation will appear in the cell.

Fig. 3-5 "STDEV" function in Excel

	A	B	C	D	E	F	G	H	I	J	K	L	M
40	422	377	359	344	356	424	345	421	423	310	359	353	381
41	328	430	384	330	376	335	401	312	305	399	352	398	343
42	389	318	431	372	383	340	383	416	379	365	411	309	312
43	326	331	420	427	346	395	434	307	419	394	344	354	374
44	358	331	314	423	426	411	303	358	374	359	353	341	333
45	348	348	321	399	460	335	343	329	335	435	422	375	322
46	303	414	318	324	387	340	412	344	323	400	327	341	333
47	375	330	378	427	343	401	321	343	420	363	395	420	367
48	367	341	321	336	340	352	398	337	401	313	358	359	352
49	338	366	306	437	407	325	302	331	338	351	398	405	302
50	329	428	418	330	314	369	369	414	405	346	339	381	390

=STDEV(A1:M50)

Things to Watch Out for When You Use Standard Deviation in Business
Relative Comparison and Standardization

How should we assess the calculated standard deviation value?

In reality, it is very difficult to use the standard deviation value by itself to discover valuable information in business, due to the following reasons.

- **Not all data is normally distributed.**

Although you cannot tell from the standard deviation how each data point is distributed (scattered or clustered together in some areas), the shape of distribution largely affects the standard deviation value.

In both **Figures 3-6 and 3-7**, all data fit within the width of 90. The shape of distribution is different, but the width of both graphs (variance) is equal.

Figure 3-6 is close to normal distribution, and the total number of values (data points) within the average±standard deviation range is close to the theoretical value of 67% (two thirds).

However, Figure 3-7 hardly looks like normal distribution. The standard deviation is larger than in Figure 3-6, but only 51% of the data lie within the average±standard deviation range. This shows that when there is a large difference in the distribution, it is difficult to assess and compare the degree of variance in data simply by using standard deviation.

Normal distribution is used to explain standard deviation in many books on statistics. It is even used in many cases in business to simplify the situation, and other types of distribution are ignored.

However, please keep in mind that you could end up with an inaccurate result if you assume a normal distribution, but the actual distribution is far from normal.

Fig. 3-6 When the actual data distribution is close to a normal distribution

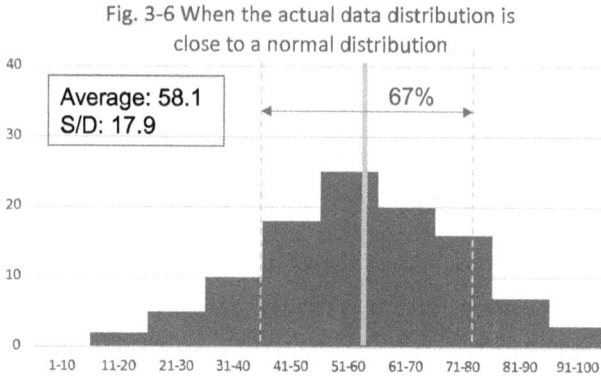

Average: 58.1
S/D: 17.9

67%

Fig. 3-7 When the actual data distribution is very different from a normal distribution

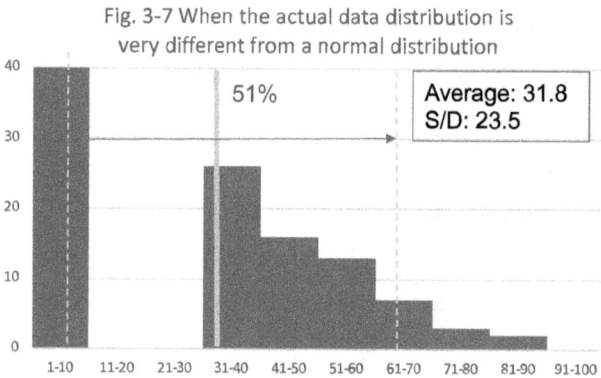

51%

Average: 31.8
S/D: 23.5

● **What does it *mean* to use standard deviation as a unit?**

What does it mean when data is X standard deviations away from the average? Even if you assume that the data is distributed normally and figure out the two thirds data range, this is useless unless there is any *meaning* to the two thirds range. Also, 95% of all data lie in the range of average value± (2×standard deviation), but this is not useful either unless there is meaning in the number 95%.

● **It is difficult to compare data with different conditions.**

Say, you counted the number of customers who came to two different stores (a large store and a small store) for a month (See **Figure 3-8**).

Obviously, having two different sized stores means that the average value and standard deviation for each store is different.

Suppose the standard deviation of the large store and small store are 223.8 and 14.6, respectively. Just because the standard deviation of the large store is larger, it does not mean that the variance is also larger. The large store has larger numbers in its data, so, even with the same degree of variance, the standard deviation automatically ends up being larger. Thus, the conditions are different for each store.

Fig. 3-8 The number of customers at a small store and a large store

Small store (customers/day)						Large store (customers/day)					
16	51	57	23	13	34	640	326	316	342	142	676
43	28	21	55	37	26	572	678	478	172	672	650
10	59	20	53	40	42	393	120	284	766	359	339
28	50	39	15	46	34	753	205	454	502	794	147
19	29	43	18	33	54	738	684	286	641	105	234
Average: 34.5						Average: 448.9					
Standard Deviation: 14.6						Standard Deviation: 223.8					

As each data is larger, S/D is also larger compared to the small store.

Let's compare a department store with an average of 10,000 customers coming in daily and a standard deviation of 600, and a family-owned store with an average of 300 customers coming in daily and a standard deviation of 150. 150 is smaller than 600, but since the total size of the data set is different (10,000 and 300), and the degree of variance is much larger for the family-owned store.

Therefore, it is meaningless to simply compare the size of the numbers 600 and 150.

Nevertheless, there is a way to utilize these numbers.

Use the same condition for a relative comparison.

Instead of comparing two different sized stores, how about comparing the number of customers at the same store for each month? Here is an example:

	July	August
Average number of customers daily	38	45
Standard deviation	12	10

This may tell you that <u>the daily number of customers is increasing, while the daily variance is decreasing each month. Thus, there is a steady increase in the number of customers</u>.

In this case, I did not assess the numerical value 12 (standard deviation) by itself. Instead, I compared numbers <u>under the same condition (same store)</u>.

It is difficult to compare standard deviation between two completely different sets of data with different sizes or shapes of distribution (e.g. the sales data of Countries A and B). However, it is useful to compare time series data on the same subject.

As I mentioned in the example of a store with average monthly sales of $50,000 (see "Standard deviation shows the stability of your business."), you can also compare the standard deviation with the average value to get a rough idea of the degree of variance.

Thus, standard deviation is useful in making relative comparisons.

You can also use it to:

- Compare the variance of the daily number of customers or sales data between stores with the same size owned by the same company.
- →The store with a larger variance may have a larger business risk.
- Check the number of units sold daily regarding the same product.

- →If variance is large, the total sales may have turned out to be large due to luck, and thus that large number is not as reliable.

- Check the monthly sales records of the same salesperson.
- →If variance is large, his/her performance may be unstable, and he/she may require additional training.

Use the standardization coefficient to compare the size or risk.

There is also an advanced method using standard deviation.

Like the example of the large and small stores, even if you have two completely different sets of data based on different conditions, you can compare how deviated each numerical value (data point) is from the average on a level playing field.

In **Figure 3-9**, the largest number of customers was 59 for the small store, and 794 for the large store. You can find out which number is more peculiar (deviated from the average) by using standard deviation to compare the numbers. In general, "peculiar = risk," and this may be deemed as a criteria of the size of the business risk. (However, not all risks are bad. Some businesses are high-risk, high-reward.)

To measure risk, calculate the standardization coefficient using this equation:

Standardization Coefficient = (Numerical Value - Average) ÷ Standard Deviation

As you can see in this equation, the standardization coefficient is the distance of a numerical value (data point) from the average in terms of how many standard deviations away it is (See **Figure 3-9**).

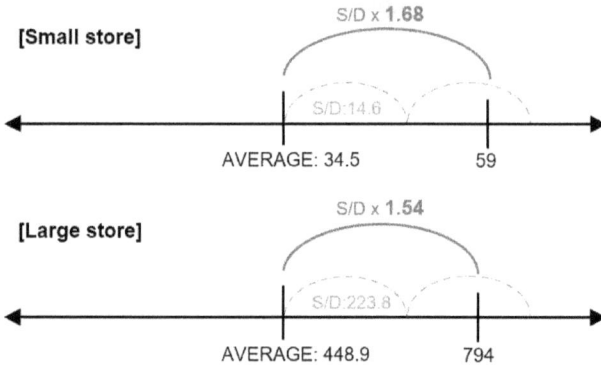

Fig. 3-9 The number of customers at a small store and a large store

Even if you have two completely different sets of data using different units, you can still compare them by converting the disparity of each numerical value (data point) from the average (variance) into how many standard deviations away they are. This conversion is called **standardization** or **normalization**.

Use the standardization coefficient to compare the number of customers that came to the small store and the large store in Figure 3-9.

	Small store	Large store
Largest number of customers	59	794
Average number of customers daily	34.5	448.9
Standard deviation	14.6	223.8
Standardization coefficient	1.68 standard deviations away	1.54 standard deviations away

Standardization Coefficient = (Numerical Value - Average) ÷ Standard Deviation

(59 - 34.5) ÷ 14.6 ≒ 1.68

(794 – 448.9) ÷ 223.8 ≒ 1.54

This shows that the degree of disparity is pretty close, and you should be able to assess data without being tricked by the size of each numerical value (data point).

Evaluate variance as a risk.

Standard deviation and standardization coefficient are not very useful in and of themselves. You need to learn how to *apply* them to produce useful information after calculating them. It is a pity that most "statistical" books only tell you how to *calculate* them and just end there.

In risk assessment, there are two ways to apply these indicators.

Application 1: Relative valuation: Compared to the other data, which one is riskier?

Compare the relative size of variance. Is it larger or smaller compared to the other data?

Variance is risk in terms of business. Large variance translates to large risk.

The word "risk" has a negative connotation in general, and it is believed that the smaller the risk, the better. However, risk not only affects your business negatively but also positively, since variance goes both ways. Not every risk is bad because there are high-risk, high-reward businesses as well.

Application 2: Estimate the impact of risk. Calculate the possible effect of variance.

Estimate how much effect variance has on the data.

This is useful when you want to know how total sales would differ due to variance in pricing, for instance.

Here is an example of Application 1.

Fig. 3-10 Sales price of a competitor's cyclonic vacuum cleaners in Country X (US$)

414	396	388	398	364	353	311	300	406	385	403	374	339	380	405
420	381	400	336	370	375	416	378	382	399	323	404	416	375	342
416	392	401	315	375	380	353	300	386	384	303	406	414	314	362
310	307	369	408	327	356	345	319	365	338	347	397	361	343	363
312	402	405	315	368	353	412	309	311	337	309	330	390	420	412
352	320	408	352	412	376	414	352	345	395	419	409	418	303	366
413	363	351	358	322	373	350	364	321	410	360	337	415	350	338
310	319	347	318	389	353	337	348	417	398	420	399	306	370	323
417	303	394	374	372	387	312	412	367	359	306	311	361	395	310
322	404	392	388	327	347	303	397	387	301	349	410	413	368	380
343	344	372	321	375	351	409	375	345	393	375	356	339	328	375
326	401	320	373	370	311	370	301	303	416	356	345	414	406	366

STDEV: 36.3   AVERAGE: 361

Figure 3-10 is the price data of 500 cyclonic vacuum cleaners sold by a competitor in Country X, from which the average price and standard deviation was calculated.

The standard deviation of $36.3 was calculated simply by using the STDEV function as discussed in "Calculate standard deviation using Excel (the STDEV function)." The average price is $361.

Since Alex's company has not entered the market in Country X, he wants to use existing data for the company's sales of cyclonic vacuum cleaners in Country Y, which is adjacent to Country X. To substitute the data of Country X with that of Country Y, Alex needs to check whether the pricing and risk of the two countries are similar, at least.

Suppose Alex collected the sales data (500 vacuum cleaners) of a competitor in Country Y for the same time period (**Figure 3-11**).

Fig. 3-11 Competitor's data in Country X and Y

	Country X	Country Y
Standard Deviation	36.3	38.1
Average	361	357

Although the data is that of a competitor, at least we can tell that there is not a large difference in the pricing and risk in both countries.

If this conclusion can be applied to Alex's company, Alex should feel more confident in using the data of his company's pricing in Country Y.

If, for instance, there is a large difference in the standard deviation (variance in pricing) even though the average price is the same for both countries, it means that there is a big difference in risk in the two markets, and the data of one of the markets should not be automatically applied to the other market.

Quantify variance to investigate its effect on business.

I have discussed the degree of variance using standard deviation. Even if you can express variance in terms of the standard deviation indicator, you also need to know how it will affect your business as a result. From the perspective of management, you need to know whether the risk is to lose $10,000 or $1,000,000 in the worst case scenario.

After calculating standard deviation, you also need to quantify the effect of variance.

If you can get a rough idea on the degree of variance, you can also reasonably imagine the worst case scenario and an average scenario.

In the next section on histograms, I will explain Application 2: how to estimate the size of the impact of risk.

Using Histograms to Visualize Variance
Getting a Full Picture of Your Data

The standard deviation value shows variance, but it does not give you a detailed image on *how* the data is scattered. It is difficult to grasp an image from numbers, not only in standard deviation and data analysis, but in general. Using **histograms** can help you visualize the data and understand how it is scattered. Histograms describe data variance in terms of "how large each numerical value (data point) is, and how many values are around the same size." Histograms display the following information on the x and y axis on a bar graph to visualize how the values are scattered.

1. **The size of each value**
2. **The total amount of values within the same size range**

The size of each value is shown on the x-axis of a histogram. Instead of plotting each value, the values are grouped into a size range, and counted within the range (this is called **"class"**). You can easily tell how many values are in each size range.

The total width of all existing data stands for the range of risk, and the total number of values inside stands for the probability of risk.

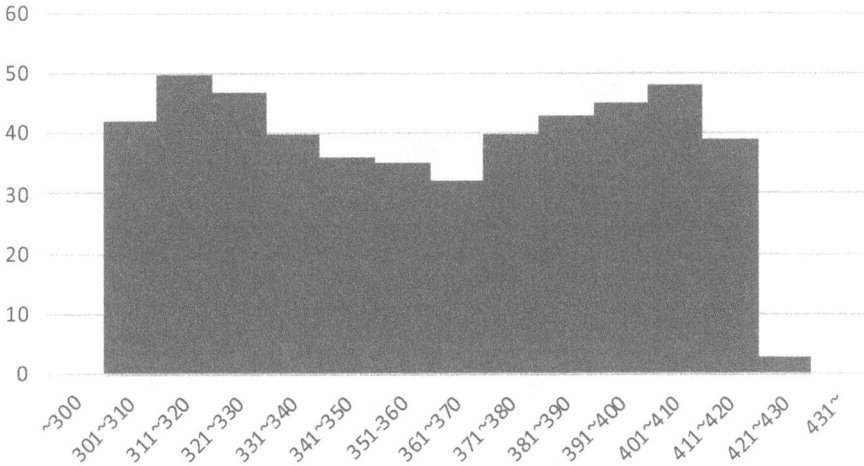

Fig. 3-12 An example of a histogram (15 classes)

In **Figure 3-12**, the range of risk is from 301 to 430, and the length of each bar shows the frequency (probability) of risk.

When you make a histogram, it is important to determine the right number of classes (bars) and the range of numbers in each class (width of each bar).

The more classes (bars) there are, the more detailed the variance would be on the graph, but it may also get too complicated to understand. On the other hand, the less classes (bars) there are, the more simplified the graph would be, and it may become hard to see how the data is distributed.

Thus, you need to choose the right number of classes (bars) so that the graph is easy to read, but at the same time, the information you can obtain from it is the most useful.

Let's make a histogram from the sales data in Country Y.

In this case, the smallest value is $303 and the largest value is $422. The data set lies within the range of $119 (= $422 - $303). (You can select the data range, and then use the MIN and MAX functions on Excel to find the smallest and largest values in the data set.)

Fig. 3-13 Another example of a histogram
(9 classes)

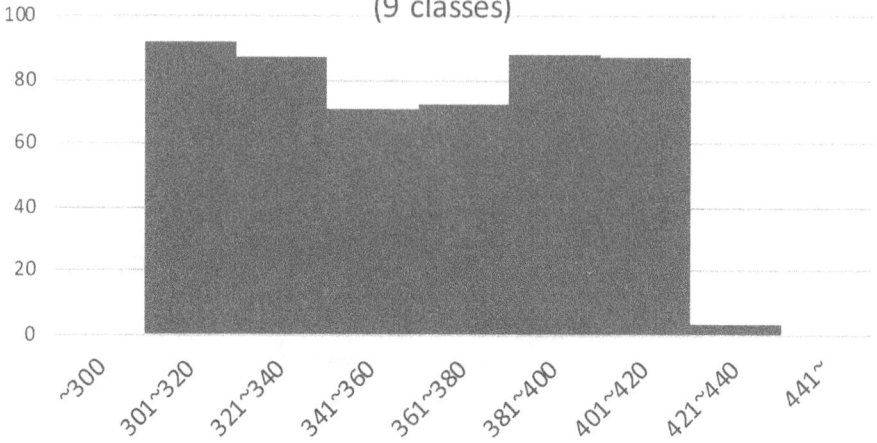

Fig. 3-14 An example of a histogram (15 classes)

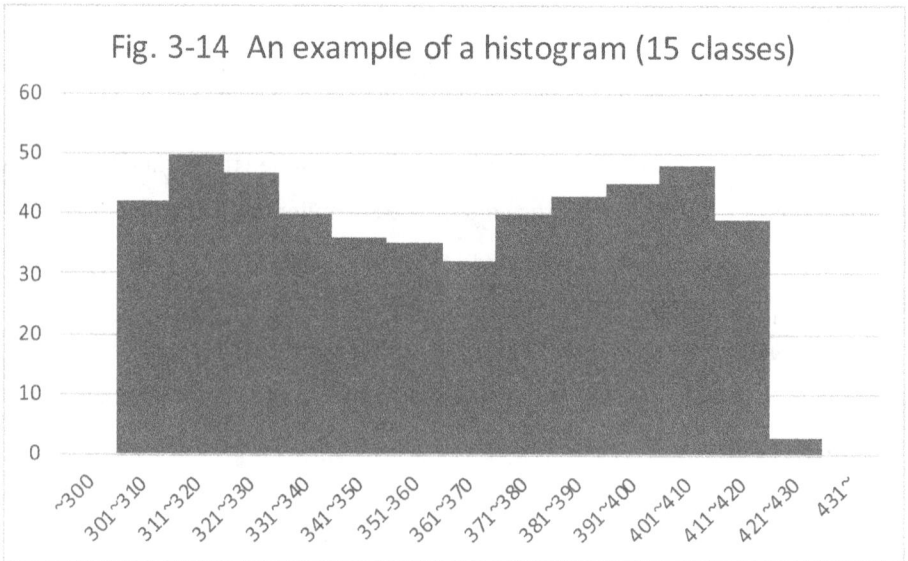

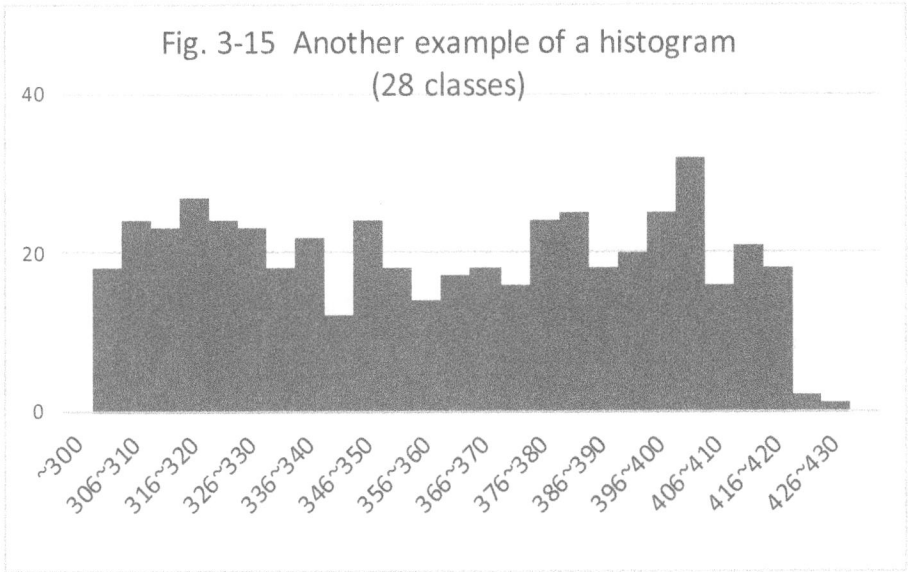

Fig. 3-15 Another example of a histogram (28 classes)

Take a look at three different histograms (**Figures 3-13 to 3-15**), each with a different number of classes; data is divided into 9, 15, or 28 classes ($20, $10, or $5 per class) respectively.

They look different, and the information that can be obtained from each graph is also different, even though the same data is used to create these graphs. In Figure 3-14, there is less data on the far left and the far right, and the bars look shorter. Meanwhile, in Figure 3-13, those characteristics are hidden due to larger class intervals. Figure 3-15 is a very detailed visualization of the variance, but it is too detailed to understand the characteristics of the data as a whole.

Of the three histograms, each having a different number of classes, which one is the most suitable for analyzing data? There is no correct answer; it depends on your objective or situation.

In Figure 3-15, the range of each bar is $5. The average value is $368. This means that the data represented by each bar is about 1.4% of the whole data set (5 ÷ 368 ≒ 0.014). How important is a 1.4% difference in pricing? In this case, it is not that important and could be seen as a margin of error. Thus, having 28 classes is a little too excessive.

Three Ideas on How to Split Data Into Classes

There are several ideas on how to determine the number of classes, of which I will introduce three of them. Suppose there are 500 values (data points) in the data set.

Idea No. 1:

Number of classes= $\sqrt{\text{(the total number of values (data points))}}$ $\rightarrow\sqrt{500} \fallingdotseq 22$

Idea No. 2:

Number of classes = 1 + LOG (the total number of values (data points)) / LOG (2) $\rightarrow 1 + \text{LOG } (500) / \text{LOG } (2) \fallingdotseq 10$

Idea No. 3:

Number of classes = 10 to 20 $\rightarrow$ constant number: 10 to 20

LOG and square root can be calculated easily by typing "LOG (the total number of values (data points))" and "= SQRT (the total number of values (data points))" respectively into cells in Excel.

Thus, if you want to make a histogram with 500 numerical values (data points), you can split the data into 22, 10, or 10 to 20 classes.

These numbers are different, but they are just reference values. Choose the most suitable number of classes depending on how reasonable it is or how organized the graph looks on a case-by-case basis. No need to get nervous. As long as you choose the number in this range, the histogram would not look that different.

Regarding the pricing in Country Y, Figure 3-14 has 15 classes (which lies right in the middle of 10 and 20). I think this graph is the most organized. What do you think?

In order to choose the right number of classes, you should compromise between a graph which is too simplified to notice any characteristics and a graph which is too detailed to look at (and to explain to the audience). It is a good idea to make several graphs and to compare them.

Figures 3-16 and 3-17 show the relation between the total number of values (data points) and classes (bins) based on Ideas No. 1 and No. 2. They show the ideal number of classes depending on the total number of values in the data set. These graphs are useful in addition to the equations above.

Fig. 3-16 Number of classes = $\sqrt{\text{(Number of data points)}}$

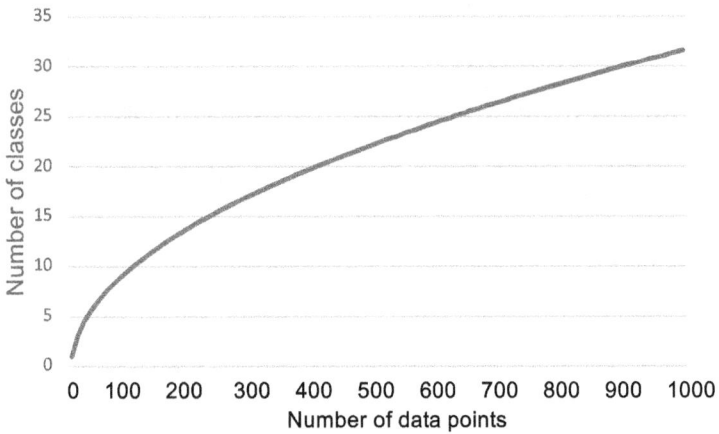

Fig. 3-17 Number of classes = 1+ LOG(Number of data points) /LOG2

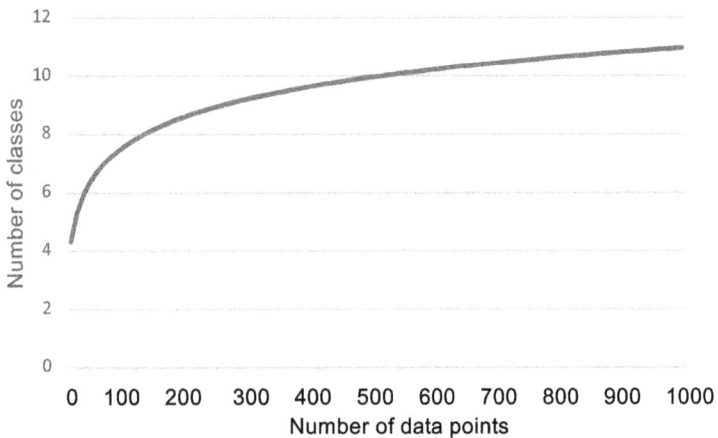

Making a Histogram Using Excel

I will show you how to make a histogram using Excel. Unfortunately, it can't be made in just one step. First, count the total number of values (data points) in each bin (class) range. Next, use that information to create a bar graph.

Preparation: Choose the numerical values where you want to split the data into classes. Type in the largest number (the boundaries) of each class, such as 290, 300, and 310... Put this data next to the actual data (**Figure 3-19**).

STEP 1: Make a frequency table to count the total number of values.

Select the "Data Analysis" Add-in on Excel. (How to get to "Data Analysis" depends on which version of Excel you are using. Please check the version.)

From the "Data Analysis" window, select "Histogram" (**Figure 3-18**).

The pop-up window shows the boxes for "Input Range", "Bin Range", and "Output Range" (Figure 3-19). In "Input Range," select the actual data range. In "Bin Range," select the data made in the "Preparation" step. Then, in "Output Range", specify the cell where you want the result to be shown. **Figure 3-20** is produced automatically as a result.

As you can see, **the frequency table** shows the total number of values (data points) in each bin (class) range.

Fig. 3-18 Histogram in "Data Analysis" Add-in

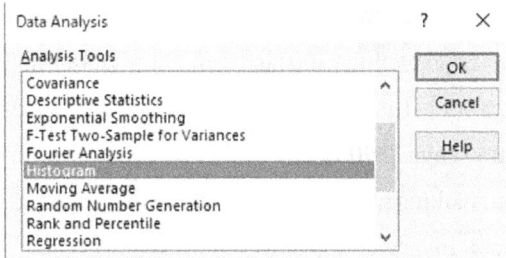

Data Analysis ? ✕

Analysis Tools
- Covariance
- Descriptive Statistics
- Exponential Smoothing
- F-Test Two-Sample for Variances
- Fourier Analysis
- Histogram
- Moving Average
- Random Number Generation
- Rank and Percentile
- Regression

OK
Cancel
Help

Fig. 3-19 Histogram in "Data Analysis" Add-in

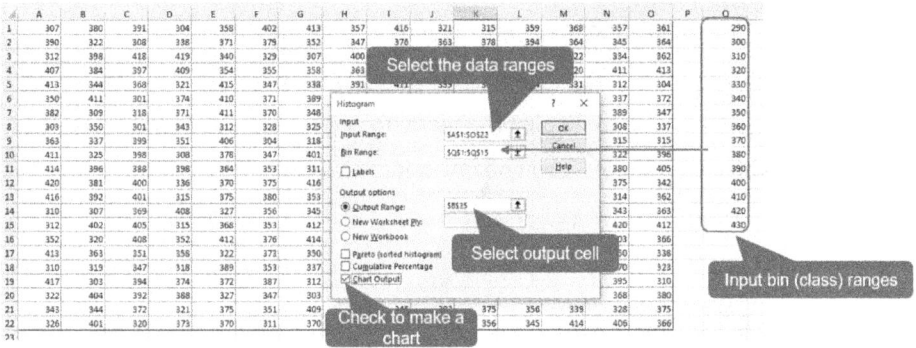

Fig. 3-19 Histogram in "Data Analysis" Add-in

Select the data ranges

Histogram ? ✕

Input
Input Range: $A$1:$Q$22
Bin Range: $Q$1:$Q$15

Labels

Output options
- Output Range: $B$15
- New Worksheet Ply:
- New Workbook
- Pareto (sorted histogram)
- Cumulative Percentage
- Chart Output

OK
Cancel
Help

Select output cell

Input bin (class) ranges

Check to make a chart

Fig. 3-20 Frequency table and graph

Bin	Frequency
290	0
300	3
310	31
320	28
330	23
340	20
350	27
360	25
370	31
380	29
390	22
400	24
410	29
420	38
430	0
More	0

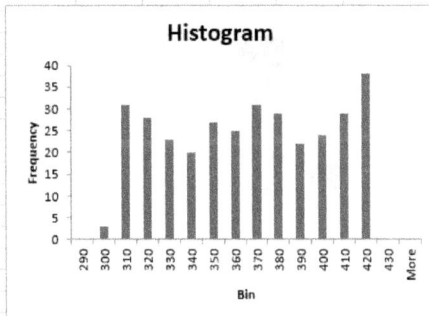

Histogram

STEP 2: Convert the frequency table into a graph.

If you use the "Data Analysis" function in Excel, the bin (class) range will be displayed with the largest value (300) instead of the data range (290 to 300). This is difficult to understand after the histogram is complete. Change the displayed value (300) to the data range (290 to 300) on the frequency table in Excel to be used as a reference when making a bar graph. Bar graphs can be made easily by using the chart wizard: select ("Insert" > "Chart").

Also, in general, the bars in histograms are adjacent to each other and are not spaced out like those in bar graphs, so you need to get rid of the spacing in between the bars. Double-click the graph and change the "Gap Width." (You can also change it by right-clicking to display the menu to select "Format Data Series." This depends on which version of Excel you are using. Please check the version.)

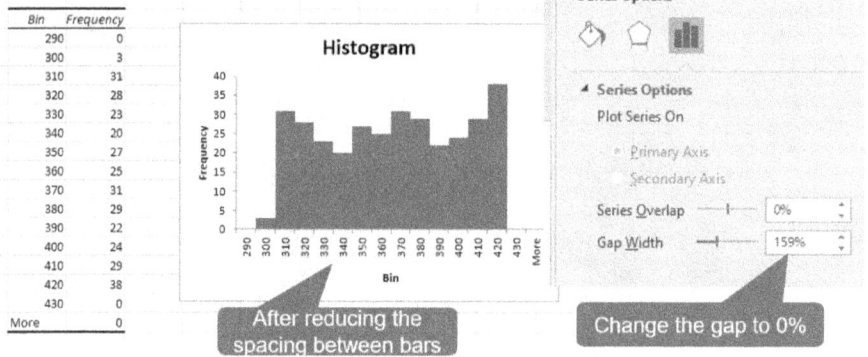

Fig. 3-21 Complete a histogram

Bin	Frequency
290	0
300	3
310	31
320	28
330	23
340	20
350	27
360	25
370	31
380	29
390	22
400	24
410	29
420	38
430	0
More	0

After reducing the spacing between bars

Format Data Series

Series Options

Series Options

Plot Series On

Primary Axis

Secondary Axis

Series Overlap — 0%

Gap Width — 159%

Change the gap to 0%

Assess upside and downside risk.

Now that Alex has completed the histogram, let's think about the impact of risk on his business plan. (Suppose similar sales and consumer activities are seen in Country X, the market Alex is trying to penetrate, and Country Y.)

Let's use Figure 3-14 (with 15 classes) again, marking the average this time (**Figure 3-22**).

Do you remember the problems with using the average explained in Chapter 2?

The average value ($368) lies within the bin (class) range ($361 to $370), which has the least number of data points (units sold). When you are told that "the average pricing is $368," you might get the wrong impression that the majority of products were sold around that price, but the average value does not necessarily guarantee that.

Although neither the average value nor the standard deviation will clarify this point, histograms will. Histograms show how each numerical value (data point) is distributed visually, making it easier to see the characteristics of the whole data set.

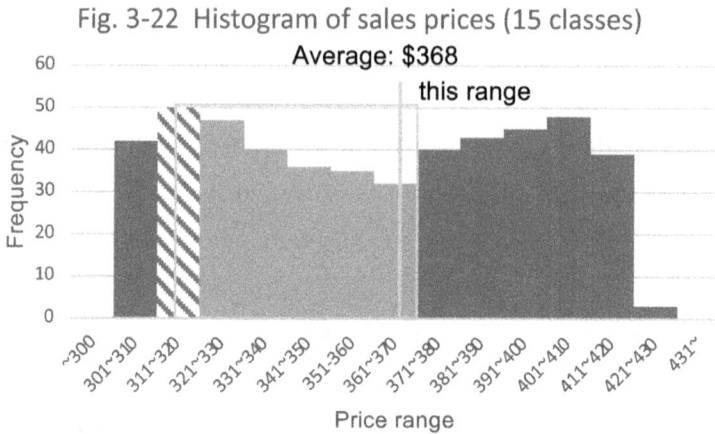

Fig. 3-22 Histogram of sales prices (15 classes)

What else can you tell from a histogram?

In general, risk consists of the impact (size) of risk and possibility.

First, let's think about the size of risk. For instance, when you look at the bin (class) ranges under the average value on the histogram, the range $311 to $320 has the most amount of data (high frequency). $315.50 lies in the middle of that range (**class value**). Let's use this as a pessimistic scenario in which the company is forced into discounting the price.

If the number of products sold were as expected, the estimated total sales would be:

$315.50 × 90,000 units ≒ about $28 million

The estimated total sales with the average value is:

$368 × 90,000 units ≒ about $33 million

This brings about a downturn of: $33 million - $28 million = $5 million
The total profit would also be smaller.

What if there were an upside? When we look at all bin (class) ranges higher than the average value on the histogram, the most frequent bin (class) range is $401 to $410 , and $405.50 is the class value. In this optimistic scenario, the estimated total sales would be:

$405.50 × 90,000 units ≒ about $36.5 million

As I mentioned, the estimated total sales with the average value is $33 million.

This brings about an upside of: $36.5 million - $33 million = $3.5 million.

"What can be proved" depends on how you read data.

The examples above show optimistic and pessimistic scenarios using classes with the most data (frequency) near the opposite ends of the histogram. Which data should be used? There are several ideas.

Fig. 3-23 How to read information from the bin (class) ranges.

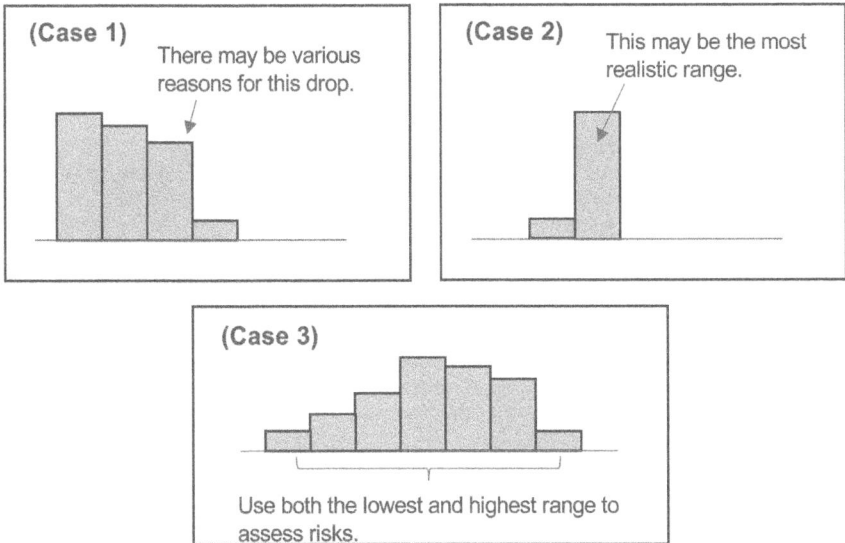

(Case 1) There may be various reasons for this drop.

(Case 2) This may be the most realistic range.

(Case 3) Use both the lowest and highest range to assess risks.

If you see a large drop in the number of data points or bar length (**Figure 3-23**, Case 1), you can choose that range to explain what is happening to a large amount of data. If there is a class with an outstanding number of data points (a long bar), you can choose that as the most realistic range, even if it is far from the average (**Figure 3-23**, Case 2). To consider a wider range of risks that are possible to a certain extent, you can also choose the lowest and highest class values ($303 and $422, **Figure 3-23**, Case 3). In general, you can give a realistic explanation using the class with the highest possibility (the largest amount of data). However, you will need to make the final decision on a case-by-case basis.

Using the downside and upside values which we calculated previously, the expected range of risk of total sales is:

$28 million < $33 million (based on average value) < $36.5 million

Instead of just concluding that "the estimated total sales amount is $33 million," now you can explain the range of risk to the audience.

Calculate the probability of risk using Excel.

Now that we discussed the size of risk (upside and downside), next, we need to know the possibility (probability) of that risk.

If the probability of a downside risk is 1%, for instance, that is not a big deal.   The possibility (probability) of risk is just as important as the size of risk.

Use the Excel functions "COUNTIF" (single criteria) and "COUNTIFS" (multiple criteria) to count the number of data points lying between $315.50 (the class value in the pessimistic scenario) and the average value "368".

Figure 3-24 is an example of how to enter data in the "COUNTIFS" function; you can enter data by hand or by selecting the data from the function.

To calculate the number of data points that are equal to or more than $315.50 and less than $368, enter: the criteria (data) range and then enter the criteria in " ".

Fig. 3-24 An example of the "COUNTIFS" function

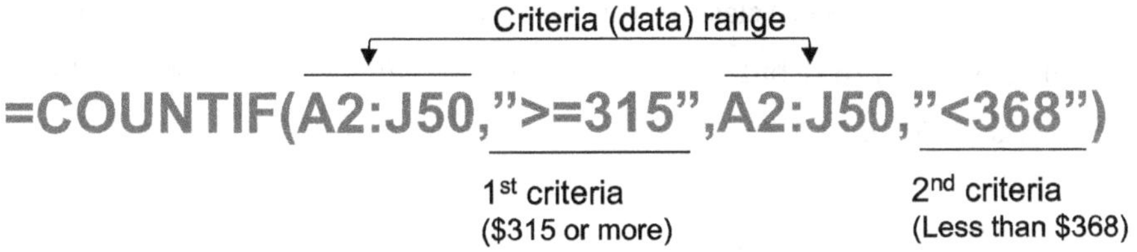

Criteria (data) range

=COUNTIF(A2:J50,">=315",A2:J50,"<368")

1st criteria
($315 or more)

2nd criteria
(Less than $368)

If you just want a rough calculation, you can count the number of data points in the class (**frequency**) by making a frequency table (see "Making a Histogram Using Excel" section).

"COUNTIFS" can be applied in many ways, not only to numbers but also to words. You can count the number of times certain words appear in the data, such as "female" (gender) or "American" (nationality).

The Possibility that the Actual Number is Lower than Average

Let's get back to Alex's data. The number of data points lying within the range in Fig. 3-24 is 257 out of 500.

$$257 \div 500 = 0.514$$

This means that about 51%, or roughly half of all data lies within the range equal to $315.50 or more, and less than the average value.

How does this look on a histogram?

On a histogram, the area of the bar graph shows probability.

The height of the bar shows the number of data points (frequency); if you add them all together, that equals the total number of data points (100%).

51% of all data lie in the rectangle labeled "This range" in the histogram (**Figure 3-22**). "This range" starts at the class value ($315.50) which lies in the middle of the $311 to $320 class, so this class is shaded. "This range" should end at the average value ($368), but it is close to $370, so I rounded it up and included the whole class ($361 to $370) in "This range."

Similarly, when calculating the possibility of upside, this was 34%. Therefore, the possibility that sales revenue in Country Y lie within the upside/downside risk range is about 85% (51%+34%), and the possibility that they may not lie within this range is about 15%.

How to assess this size and probability of risk will be determined by management case-by-case.

In this case, we based our calculation on the sales data of Country Y. Keep in mind that this premise may not necessarily be applicable to other markets. (When we are focused on calculating numbers accurately, we tend to forget that our analysis is based on certain premises or limitations.)

In most situations, we don't have perfect data, conditions nor premises (as shown in Alex's example).

In planning for an uncertain future, don't rely on just one numerical value (e.g. the average), but also assess risk for better decision making.

Standard deviation and histograms will help you quantify variance and assess risk.

Practical Examples: How to Use Standard Deviation in Business

Here are some specific ideas on how you can use standard deviation in business.

- Visualize the variance in data which cannot be seen in the average value.
  1. Eliminate irregular situations (e.g. a large tour group that shopped in bulk at the store) and find out the average number of customers daily.
  2. If you are reporting the average value of sales figures, but are not sure if this number can be achieved constantly, you can prove that the standard deviation is large and the business is not stable enough to maintain that number constantly.

- Find out whether the values (data points) are scattered or close together.

  If you have a large amount of data, you can find out the average easily using Excel, but the average does not tell you how the numbers are scattered. Try using standard deviation instead to find this out.

- Prove that the data points are scattered.

  Many people assume from the average value that a lot of values (data points) exist near the average value, and it is difficult to explain how scattered the actual data is. To clarify this matter, you can use standard deviation to show the large variance and explain that there is a risk.

- Verify the risks that cannot be understood from the average.

  You can verify the risks or facts that cannot be understood from the average value. It is also useful when you want to check whether the person presenting the average is making the audience shift their focus away from the facts.

- Is the analysis presentable?

    Your analysis would be much more insightful and presentable if you use the standard deviation instead of just ending the discussion with the average.

- Your instincts tell you otherwise.

    Even after calculating the average, your instincts may tell you otherwise, especially when the majority of the data is distributed near the smallest and/or the largest values instead of the average value. This can be confirmed if the standard deviation is large. The standard deviation is more objective and convincing than your instincts.

Using data analysis, Alex investigated the expected risk and the number of units that need to be sold to achieve his goal. Alex finally got the big picture of the business plan.

Alex: "The estimated sales are from $28 million to $36.5 million. Now I know how to describe risk using numbers. With standard deviation and histograms, I can visualize data."

At first, Alex didn't have a specific image of how he was going to make the business plan. By using numbers to describe the business, he was able to put his thoughts into shape.

COLUMN: USING THE "STDEVP FUNCTION" WHEN YOU'RE WORKING WITH THE ENTIRE DATA SET

There are two functions in Excel to calculate standard deviation: the STDEV and STDEVP functions. The STDEVP function is used when the data you are using is the whole data set (population).

Say, you want to use the data of second grade students at a certain elementary school (sample) to analyze the characteristics of second grade students in the entire nation (population). It is not realistic to collect and analyze all data in the population, so the sample data is used instead. If there is a limited data range that can be analyzed and deemed as the population, it is not treated as a sample but as the whole population. In real life, this difference will not make much difference, though (especially when there are a large number of data points).

You can calculate standard deviation using the following equations. The difference in the two equations is the denominator. If the data used in the calculation is a sample, the denominator is the total number of values (data points) – 1.

Even with the same variance, if the total number of data points is smaller, the denominator is smaller, leading to a larger standard deviation.

Population standard deviation (STDEVP) = $\sqrt{\dfrac{\text{the sum of (value of a data point} - \text{average value})^2}{\text{the total number of data points}}}$

Sample standard deviation (STDEV) = $\sqrt{\dfrac{\text{the sum of (value of a data point} - \text{average value})^2}{\text{the total number of data points} - 1}}$

Chapter 4

What is the success factor?

—Correlation Analysis: Using Data to Predict the Future

Using Past Data to Plan Ahead

Alex: "I can finally see the goal. When I was given this assignment—to create this business plan—I wasn't sure what to do in the beginning. Now that I know the size of the market and the risks in sales, I can utilize data to put ideas into shape. My arguments are starting to sound convincing. I have a feeling the presentation is going to be a success."

Boss: "Wait a minute. We tend to focus too much on what we're working on and lose sight of things. Step back and look at the big picture. What can you prove right now? Is anything still missing?"

Alex: "...Missing?"

Boss: "Yes. We've been collecting past data to grasp the situation, remember? If you show this to the audience, it's just going to be a report on *what's been happening*. We still need to make a business plan that shows *what we will do in the future*."

Alex: "Hmm...That's true...I don't have anything close to a plan yet."

Boss: "A plan is not something that magically appears when you collect information or do research. It needs to describe *what you want to do*. If you're going to explain that there is a risk in your business, you need to plan how you're going to avoid it. To create a good plan, you should be able to say 'Although there is a negative risk, I have an idea to keep this from happening, which is... This is going to work because...'"

Alex: "Wow, that sounds difficult, but I understand what you mean. I can't just analyze past data to explain the current status and submit that as a plan. *What I want to do.*' Do I show that with data and numbers?"

Boss: "Of course! Inspiration and perseverance can help you, but they are not enough to make a convincing presentation for management decisions. To plan for the future, you'd still use past data, but this time, you need to *think differently*."

Alex could hardly keep up with what his boss was saying. He gave her a confused look so she might give him more advice.

Boss: "For example, we sell our products in other markets. We already tried several sales strategies and have examples of success and failure. You can use that information."

Alex: "Yes, I found information on past sales promotions with the sales data for each market. Oh, wait... I know what kinds of promotions were implemented, but I don't know how effective they were...Which of them were successful? Can I still use this data? I don't want all this to go to waste."

> ## Which promotional strategy is the most effective?
> *Use correlation to give meaning to data.*

In the previous chapter, we looked into the risks such as change in pricing that could interfere with your target sales and profit. What, then, can be done to avoid the risks?

After speaking with the boss, Alex knew he had to do something to avoid the risks, but he felt stuck trying to come up with a convincing proposal on what measures should be taken. He was familiar with popular types of sales promotions: TV commercials, newspaper and magazine ads, online ads, discount coupons to be used on the next purchase, sales incentives for the shop, and so on; however, he had no idea how effective any of them were.

In addition, he had to maximize the effectiveness of the promotion within the budget limitations of the company.

When there are too many things to think about, you need to organize your thoughts and focus on what you are trying to achieve.

"I want to avoid negative risks as much as possible, and think of ways to achieve good sales results."
"However, the company has budget limitations."
"Thus, I need to make sure that the money spent leads to effective results."

The most important point is that there needs to be a connection between the money spent and effectiveness.

Once you discover the connection (relationship) between money spent and the effectiveness of each strategy, you will understand what to spend money on.

Quantify the connection with data.

You can use statistical methods to quantify the strength of the relationship between two data sets.

When asked whether there is a relationship, realistically speaking, you cannot answer with a straight "yes" or "no." If you rely only on your instincts and experience, you might say "Newspaper ads are meaningless," or "Flyers are very effective." These statements cannot be compared and tested; you will end up with an unproductive discussion. However, if you can quantify the strength of the relationship between data sets, you can compare and analyze different combinations from an objective point of view.

This relationship between data sets is called **"correlation."** Quantifying a relationship statistically may sound very hard, and though it is difficult to completely understand the statistical theory, correlation analysis is just as easy as calculating the average or standard deviation if you use Excel.

Find information from a pair of data sets.

Before getting to quantification, I want to discuss the difference between correlation and the previously mentioned average and standard deviation.

In the previous chapters, we only looked at one data set at a time (e.g. pricing) and explained its characteristics with statistical indicators like the average value and standard deviation to be used in calculation.

With correlation, we will analyze **two data sets**.

By looking at the relationship between two data sets, you can obtain more information than when you just use one data set. This new information is not a characteristic of either individual data set, but can only be discovered by pairing two data sets.

When you only have one data set, you can only compare such things as the size of the numbers within the data set. With two data sets, you can understand the relationship between the data, e.g. "how the value A associates with the other value B."

Another important point in using correlation is that each factor in the two data sets needs to **be paired**.

What does it mean for the factors to be paired?

Figure 4-1 shows the History and Mathematics test scores of thirty students numbered 1 to 30. The test scores for both subjects of each individual student are placed side-by-side, so the two data are paired.

On the other hand, **Figure 4-2** shows random test scores, and the scores near each other are not necessarily from the same student. Thus, the scores are not paired.

In such a case, you cannot find correlation between the two data sets.

Fig. 4-1 Students' test scores **(When the two data sets are paired)**

Student No.	History	Math	Student No.	History	Math	Student No.	History	Math
1	79	76	11	66	75	21	39	86
2	43	36	12	38	64	22	90	100
3	50	71	13	53	76	23	98	72
4	31	78	14	73	57	24	71	68
5	32	40	15	82	89	25	96	68
6	64	73	16	73	97	26	62	52
7	69	45	17	51	42	27	99	91
8	64	52	18	45	86	28	88	82
9	69	32	19	70	66	29	48	73
10	35	69	20	37	91	30	61	37

Fig. 4-2 Students' test scores **(When the two data sets are not paired)**

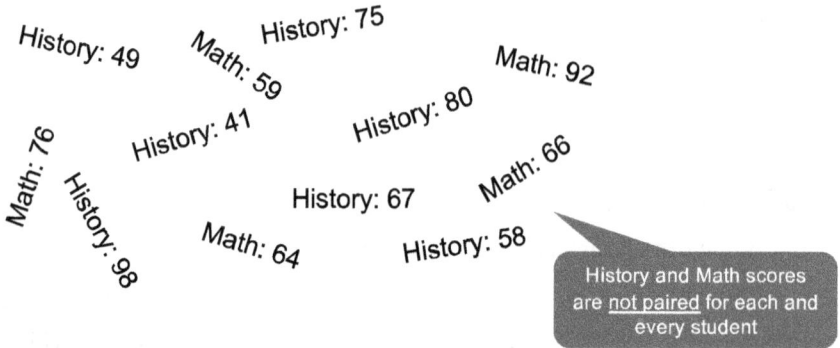

In my experience, most data used in business are paired. Here is an example of paired monthly data: expenses in April (Data X) and number of products sold in April (Data Y).

There are also other types of paired data like the population and sales in each country. In most cases, you can find paired data.

The correlation coefficient indicates the strength of correlation.

Let's look at some examples of correlation analysis.

Strictly speaking, correlation shows the proportionality of two data sets.

Do you remember studying proportion in school? Data "y" and Data "x" are proportional when **y=mx+b**, in which "m" and "b" are constants.

A **positive correlation** exists between variables "x" and "y" if "m" is a positive value and an increase in "x" results in an increase in "y". If the variables have a **negative correlation**, "m" will be a negative value, and "y" will decrease as "x" increases.

Correlation can be strong or weak, depending on how much the change in one data set affects a change in the other data set.

This strength or weakness of the relationship between the two data sets is measured with an indicator called **"correlation coefficient."** The correlation coefficient lies within the numerical range from -1 to +1, depending on whether the two data sets move in the same direction or in opposite directions. If the correlation coefficient is a positive value, it is a **positive correlation** (both data sets increase or decrease together). The closer the correlation coefficient is to 1, the stronger the positive correlation is. +1 stands for a completely proportional relationship, while 0 means that there is no correlation (See **Figure 4-3**).

On the other hand, in a **negative correlation**, the two data sets move in opposite directions (one data set increases while the other one decreases), showing a negative correlation coefficient; the closer it is to -1, the stronger the negative correlation is.

Fig. 4-3 The correlation coefficient is an indicator that measures the strength and direction of the correlation.

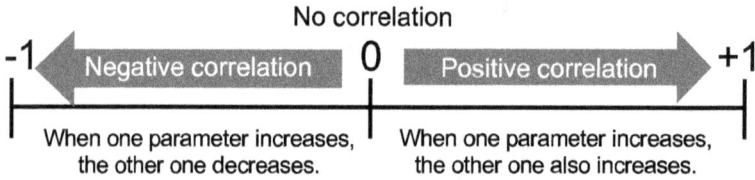

No correlation

-1 Negative correlation 0 Positive correlation +1

When one parameter increases, the other one decreases.

When one parameter increases, the other one also increases.

Correlation Between the Spread of the Flu and the Waiting Time of Pediatric Patients

Let's look at an example.

Say, the average waiting time of pediatric patients during flu season was recorded every week. The waiting time should vary depending on the season and/ or any other types of diseases that are also spreading. (The day of the week and time of day could also affect the waiting time.)

You can check the information on the spread of the flu on government websites (e.g. CDC in the U.S.). The indicator of the spread of diseases and the waiting time of pediatric patients tend to correlate. If one data increases (decreases) and the other data increases (decreases) with it, even if they are not completely proportional, it means that there is a (positive) correlation. In this case, the correlation coefficient is likely to be a value from 0 to 1 and closer to 1.

The difference in units or the size of numerical values in the two data sets do not matter in correlation analysis. Like the example shown above, you can combine any two types of data as we are only looking at how strong the proportional relationship of the numerical values is.

Correlation analysis can be applied in infinite ways. Theoretically, you can use whatever combination you want as long as you have two data sets.

Calculate the correlation coefficient using Excel (the CORREL Function).

The equation to calculate the **correlation coefficient** uses the square root and is a little complicated. Realistically, you do not need to know this equation in business, so I will skip it and show you how to calculate it using Excel in seconds.

The **"CORREL function"** in Excel is used to calculate the correlation coefficient.

Select a cell and type **"=CORREL"** (or select this from the function options), and in the parentheses, select the cells including two data sets as input. That is all you need to do!

In **Figure 4-4**, I typed in the function and pushed the Enter key, and the correlation coefficient 0.95 was shown in the selected cell.

The value 0.95 proves that there is a very strong correlation between the two data sets.

Fig. 4-4 CORREL function in Excel

38	36	53
39	7	2
40	5	8
41	16	39
42		
43	=CORREL(A2:A41,B2:B41)	
44		

Fig. 4-5 Visualized correlation

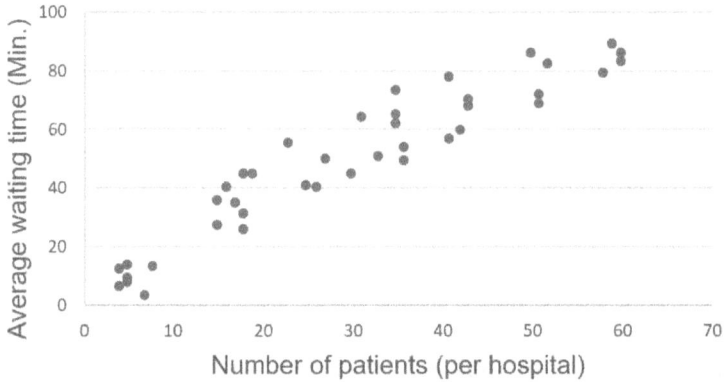

Now, let's visualize the two data sets.

In **Figure 4-5**, the average waiting time at pediatricians' offices is shown on the y-axis, and the number of patients waiting per hospital is shown on the x-axis. This graph, with two factors of the data displayed on the x and y axes, is called a **"scatter diagram."** You can easily make a scatter diagram by selecting it from the "Charts" button in Excel.

What information can be obtained from the scatter diagram?

Figure 4-5 looks very similar to a linear function graph with an upward trend; an increase on the x-axis results in an increase on the y-axis, meaning that there is a positive correlation. In other words, a graph with an upward trend shows a positive relationship, and the linearity shows how proportional the two data sets are.

The dots are not plotted in a perfect line, and some dots are scattered away from the line. The two data sets are not perfectly correlated; however, they are positively correlated to some degree.

This "degree," described numerically, is the correlation coefficient.

The magnitude of the correlation coefficient determines correlation.

What, then, is the minimum value of a correlation coefficient to prove whether two data sets are correlated or not?

When the correlation coefficient is close to 1 (e.g. 0.95), the data sets are obviously correlated. In reality, however, you may not be able to determine this so easily.

Unfortunately, there is no clear-cut threshold to determine whether data sets are correlated or not.

The following standards have often been used, and I like to set 0.7 as my threshold (There are different opinions on this).

Correlation Coefficient

-1 to -0.7	Strong negative correlation
-0.7 to -0.5	Negative correlation
-0.5 to 0.5	No correlation
0.5 to 0.7	Positive correlation
0.7 to 1	Strong positive correlation

It is easier to understand these numbers when they are visualized onto scatter diagrams. **Figure 4-6** illustrates scatter diagrams for the correlation coefficients 0, 0.40, 0.70 and 0.90.

Fig. 4-6 Scatter Diagrams With Different Correlation Coefficients

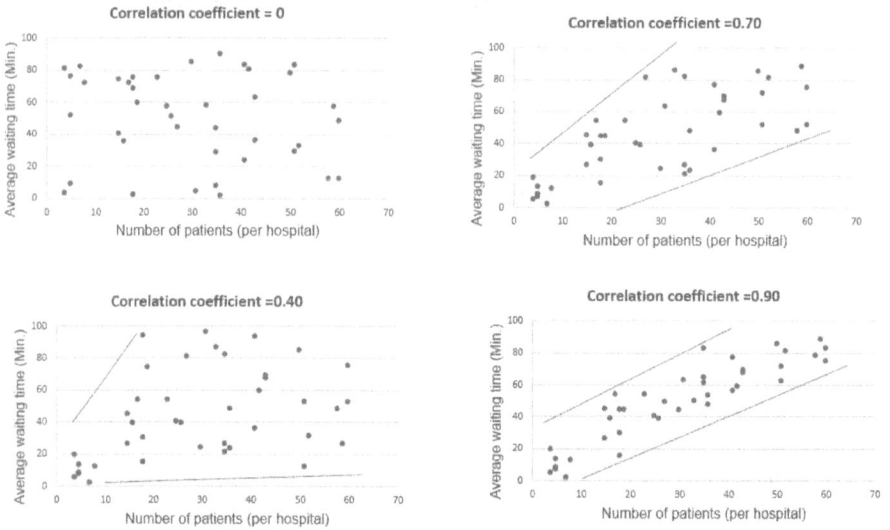

When the correlation coefficient is 0.4, your audience may not agree that the scatter diagram shows a strong upward trend. More people would agree as it approaches 0.9.

Figure 4-7 shows scatter diagrams with negative correlations.

When the value on the y-axis decreases as the value on the x-axis increases, the graph will have a downward trend.

The size of the correlation coefficient and the variance of data work in the same way as positive correlation.

Fig. 4-7 Negative correlations

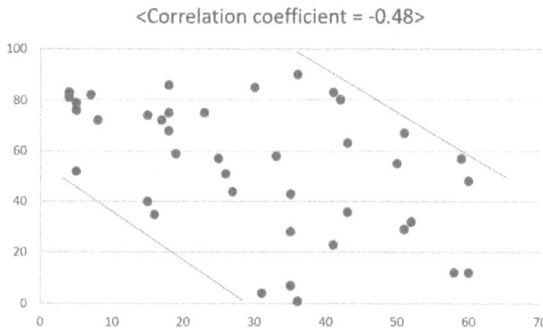

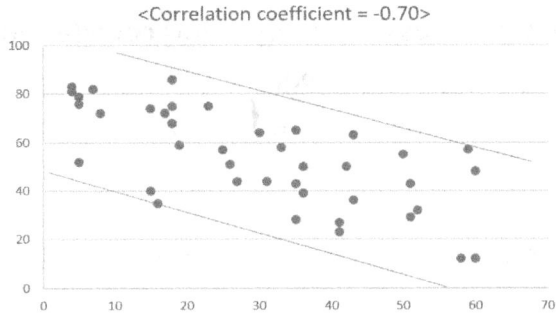
<Correlation coefficient = -0.70>

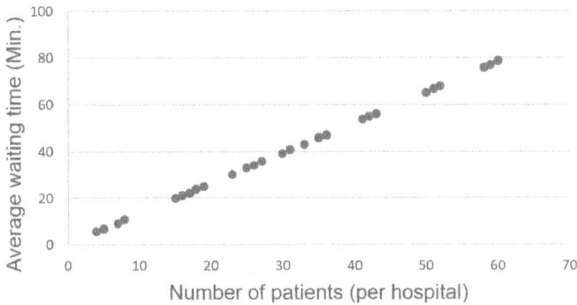
Fig. 4-8 Perfect positive correlation

If the two data are perfectly correlated, that means they are completely proportional. Thus, the scatter diagram would look like a linear graph (y=mx+b) as shown in **Figure 4-8**.

In this case, the correlation coefficient is +1. I have never seen data with perfect correlation like this in real life. If such a correlation existed, it would be clear-cut and you would not need to analyze the relationship.

The correlation coefficient may be a boring numerical value, but you can have a better idea of the strength of the relationship by visualizing it with a scatter diagram. This information is reassuring when used in conjunction with the correlation coefficient, making your argument more convincing and understandable to your audience.

> # Determine the success factor by using correlation.
> *What is the most effective promotional strategy?*

How effective is each strategy (What is the output)?

Correlation seems simple at first, but because it is so simple, it can be applied in many ways.

Let's look at Alex's example.

Alex wants an effective promotional strategy since a large amount of money is going to be invested.

If he finds out the strength of the relationship (correlation) between how much money is invested and how effective a strategy is, he can decide which strategy to invest in. At the very least, he would not want to waste money on a strategy that is not correlated at all, or has a weak correlation with how much money is spent.

Whatever the case may be, he would need to quantify information into numerical data so that it could be analyzed.

Money is expressed with numbers, but how can you express the effectiveness of a strategy with numbers?

In business, sales strategies are used to produce final output (sales, profit, etc.). Therefore, you need to choose the right output.

Which indicator (data) will be used to express the output of each strategy? Can the data be monitored, and is it obtainable? Think carefully.

For instance, if you are planning to use a newspaper ad, <u>what will be the direct output?</u> Examples of output may be the number of customers that came to the store, or the percentage increase in sales, etc.

Choose directly-related data to obtain a more accurate analysis result.

Sales and profit are obviously the final output, but before getting there, there are interim outputs such as increasing brand value and customer satisfaction, cutting costs, and increasing the number of customers coming to the stores, all of which would help you achieve your final output.

In general, <u>if several factors affect the final output, or if there are several interim outputs before reaching the final output, they will interfere with the correlation analysis.</u>

Say, you obtained data on the number of service staff at an electronics store, and data on total sales. There may be a correlation and the number of staff may affect total sales. However, other factors may also be at play.

To find out only the effectiveness of increasing the number of staff, you can analyze its correlation with the number of waiting customers, their waiting time or customer satisfaction and such, which are more directly related to the number of staff than they are to sales (**Figure 4-9**).

Therefore, to calculate the correlation accurately, it is ideal that the two data sets are directly related (there are no other factors interfering with the results). (In reality, it is impossible to find two data sets with zero influence from any other factors unless you artificially create them.)

Fig. 4-9 Direct correlation

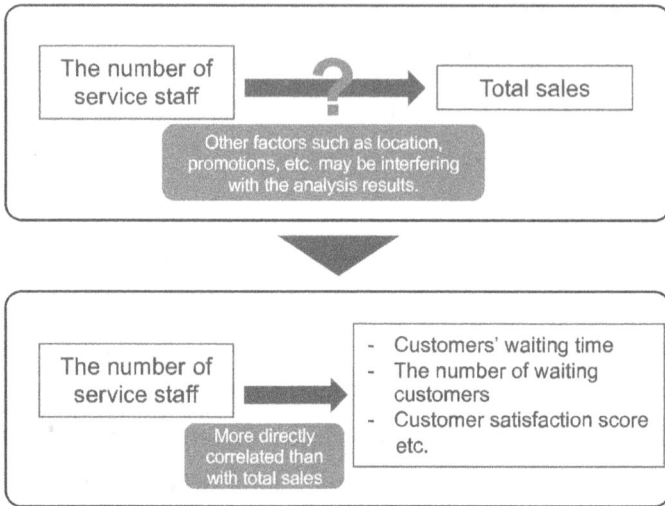

The Most Effective Sales Strategy

Alex found different sales strategies implemented in Country Y, but could not find data showing how effective each promotion was (The effectiveness was not monitored.). Thus, he chose sales as the output.

He suddenly noticed that Country Y was a vast country, and three area sales managers divided the country into three areas in which they each used a different strategy.

This was good news because he could look into each area separately within the same market. If he only knew that different strategies were used simultaneously in the same country, it would have been impossible to find out which strategy generated the most sales. In analysis, you should avoid situations where several different factors affect one output at the same time.

The three managers each invested in the following strategies that they thought were effective within their budget limitations.

Area	Strategy
Area A	Online ads
Area B	Discount coupons (for customers who purchased products, to be used on the next purchase)
Area C	In-store events

Figure 4-10 shows the monthly expenditure on promotions during the previous year, and the monthly sales of cyclonic vacuum cleaners in each area. (Please note that data on sales and expenditure are paired using the "monthly" attribute.)

Fig. 4-10 Sales promotion data in **Country Y**

Area A

Online ads	Jan.	Feb.	Mar.	Apr.	May	Jun.	Jul.	Aug.	Sep.	Oct.	Nov.	Dec.
Sales revenue ($000)	105	178	200	98	170	138	198	245	175	80	143	190
Expenditure ($000)	12	32	5	15	21	32	45	17	0	21	34	30

Area B

Discount coupons	Jan.	Feb.	Mar.	Apr.	May	Jun.	Jul.	Aug.	Sep.	Oct.	Nov.	Dec.
Sales revenue ($000)	93	188	283	113	148	238	258	195	223	135	78	230
Expenditure ($000)	0	14	55	9	39	48	55	41	45	3	3	49

Area C

In-store events	Jan.	Feb.	Mar.	Apr.	May	Jun.	Jul.	Aug.	Sep.	Oct.	Nov.	Dec.
Sales revenue ($000)	41	189	288	267	71	147	249	182	24	182	92	51
Expenditure ($000)	12	33	3	31	3	4	13	3	0	28	20	7

The correlation coefficients of the sales revenue and expenditure of each area are as follows:

Area	Promotional strategy	Correlation coefficient
Area A	Online ads	0.07
Area B	Discount coupons	0.90
Area C	In-store events	0.36

Alex analyzed the data and found that there was a strong correlation between sales and discount coupons and concluded <u>that customers who purchase cyclonic vacuum cleaners respond well to discount coupons, and that the company should focus investing in this type of sales promotion.</u>

In-store events may also help, but discount coupons have a stronger impact, considering how the amount of money spent affects the effectiveness of the strategy (In other words, there is a strong correlation).

In this simplified analysis, the output is *monthly* sales revenue. In real life, though, other factors may affect sales, such as *seasonal fluctuations* (Holiday shopping or year-end bonuses may boost sales).

In such cases, you can **process data** (see Chapter 1) by converting the absolute values in the sales data to year-over-year data to compare the difference or ratio. By comparing the data with the data of the previous year (when there were no promotions), factors such as seasonal fluctuations will not affect the comparison, and you can find out whether the promotion directly affected sales.

Things to Watch Out for in Dealing With Correlation

You can use Excel to easily calculate correlation within seconds. Correlation is shown with a number between -1 and +1. It is a very useful analysis method that is pretty straightforward and easy to understand. I like to pair two data sets and analyze the correlation just to see what happens.

Sometimes, I find a strong correlation which I never imagined before the analysis. I get curious whether it is just a coincidence or if there is a surprising connection between the data sets. (In some cases, I dig deeper and find valuable information.)

As you can see, correlation analysis can be done easily by anyone, but there are things to watch out for. In correlation analysis, any data set can be analyzed to produce a result, even if the way you utilize the data or the premise of the analysis is wrong.

In such a case, Excel and analysis results do not give you an alert that you are making a mistake. The person analyzing the data needs to notice the risk and watch out for an inaccurate (or even an incorrect) result. Please read the following guide.

Are the combinations of data reasonable? Think carefully.

Let's look at Alex's analysis result once again (Figure 4-10). Alex followed the analysis procedures and his calculations were correct, from which he concluded that money should be invested heavily on discount coupons.

However, when you look more carefully at the data, it is clear that online ads do not necessarily have a direct influence on customers' purchasing behavior in the same way that discount coupons and in-store events do. Ads keep appearing for a set period of time, and they needs to be shown repeatedly until the company brand becomes well-known. There could also be a time lag between the customers' seeing the advertisements and being informed about the products, and their subsequent purchase.

Let's assume that it takes a month for the ads to effectively lure customers into buying the products and generate sales.

Under this assumption, each sales data should be paired with each data for expenditure on online ads from a month ago for use in correlation analysis (e.g. January expenditure pairs with sales in February. See **Figure 4-11**).

Fig. 4-11 Sales promotion data in **Country Y (One-month gap)**

Area A

Online ads	Jan.	Feb.	Mar.	Apr.	May	Jun.	Jul.	Aug.	Sep.	Oct.	Nov.	Dec.
Sales revenue ($000)	105	178	200	98	170	138	198	245	175	80	143	190
Expenditure ($000)	12	32	5	15	21	32	45	17	0	21	34	30

This time, the correlation coefficient is 0.88, which is pretty high. If this time lag for the effectiveness of the ads is reasonable, Alex would not have ruled out the use of ads.

This analogy was reached by *thinking carefully*.

The analyst needs to pause and think instead of jumping straight into using the data.

Fake Correlation and Cause and Effect

Not every correlation should be used to produce an analysis result. Even if you find a strong correlation between two data sets, they may not be directly related.

1. Coincidence (Both data happen to have a similar trend.)

If stock prices kept plummeting last week, and the average temperature kept dropping due to the season simultaneously, the correlation coefficient between the two data may turn out high. Nevertheless, there is obviously no theoretical connection between the two data sets.

2. Data That Are Simply Related to Each Other

For instance, height and weight, age and size of feet are obviously related and there is no significance in discovering the correlation.

3. Spurious Correlation

A **spurious correlation** is a mathematical relationship between two data sets which appear causal from the calculations, but in truth, other factors affect the results and make it seem like there is a connection.

Figure 4-12 shows an example with two data: annual salary and the time people get up every morning. You may see a correlation and think that a person who earns a higher salary gets up earlier than others because some people have this stereotype. However, don't assume that this causal relationship is thus proved.

Fig. 4-12 Does a person who earns a higher salary get up earlier?

It's unlikely that these two factors are correlated with each other, but the analysis result may indicate a spurious correlation.

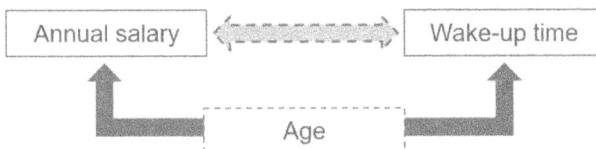

Annual salary ⟵░░░░░░░⟶ Wake-up time

Age

Other hidden factors may affect the correlation, such as age. Some companies have seniority-based pay systems in which employees who worked in the company for a shorter amount of time (They tend to be younger.) are paid less than those who worked longer (They tend to be older.). Age also affects the time you get up in the morning; older people tend to get up earlier than younger people. Thus, age may be correlated with both your annual salary and wake-up time, giving you a result that appears to be a correlation between annual salary and wake-up time, even if these two factors may not be directly related to each other.

This fake correlation **(spurious correlation)** may be easy to notice when someone points it out to you, but it is difficult to find it on your own because the third factor is hidden and will not appear as data. You need to take a guess by looking at the correlation between the data and other factors (e.g. age) and think carefully.

It is not realistic to look into any and all possible spurious correlations and to confirm the truth for every single one of them. What is important is that spurious correlation does exist, and to be a keen observer while you do your analysis.

4. Correlation Due to a Third Factor

This is another type of spurious correlation. Take a look at **Figure 4-13**. If you do not notice the fact that you overate because you felt hungrier from jogging, you might immediately draw the conclusion that you gained weight only from jogging.

Fig. 4-13 Does jogging cause weight gain?

It's unlikely that these two factors are correlated with each other, but the analysis result may indicate a spurious correlation.

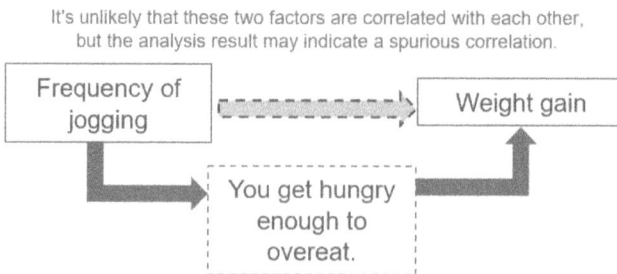

5.   How to Check Whether There Is a Cause and Effect Relationship

Correlation does not necessarily mean that there is a cause and effect relationship. However, we tend to try to make things sound more reasonable than they actually are and get comfortable with this idea, immediately jumping to the conclusion that there is a cause and effect in the seemingly correlated data. There is a greater risk of misunderstanding the data if you connect the background information and make up a story in your mind, or make an assumption instead of confirming the truth.

It is quite common for people to automatically assume that there is a cause and effect relationship because they see a correlation between the two data sets. For instance, global warming is a well-known phenomenon in which a correlation has been found between carbon dioxide (CO_2) and temperature, but cause and effect between the two data sets has yet to be found.

It is very difficult to confirm the cause and effect relationship of two data that are correlated, but here are some tips that may help you (They are somewhat helpful but I cannot guarantee that they work all the time).

a.   **Point in Time**

Check the point in time, since cause always comes before effect. Does the sequence of events make sense?

b.   **Generality**

If there is a strong cause and effect relationship, you should reach a similar analysis result even when you change the attributes (e.g. time or place), conditions, or environment. Change the conditions several times and compare the results.

c.   **Threshold**

In some cause and effect relationships, when one data (cause) surpasses a certain value (threshold), it affects the other data (effect). Check whether your data has this characteristic. For instance, if electricity (air conditioner) usage surges when the temperature reaches 86°F (30°C), it is reasonable to believe that there is a cause and effect relationship between temperature and electricity usage.

None of the three ideas explained above are perfect. Please note that you are using data to make business decisions, not to write an academic paper. If everyone believes that there is a cause and effect relationship, and your gut is telling you that it is true, you might as well agree and move on to the next step.

6. Don't switch the cause and effect factors!

Even when there is a cause and effect relationship, you need to be careful how you interpret information.

In **Figure 4-14**, which factor is the cause — employee satisfaction or corporate performance?

Fig. 4-14 What comes first, employee satisfaction or corporate performance?

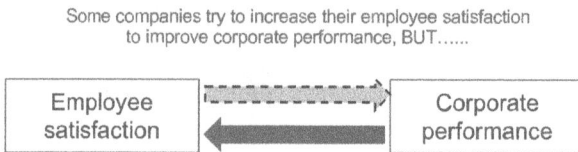

Some companies try to increase their employee satisfaction to improve corporate performance, BUT......

| Employee satisfaction | | Corporate performance |

The cause→effect arrow might be pointing in the wrong direction. Due to high corporate performance, employees might get a raise or a bonus, and be more satisfied with their jobs.

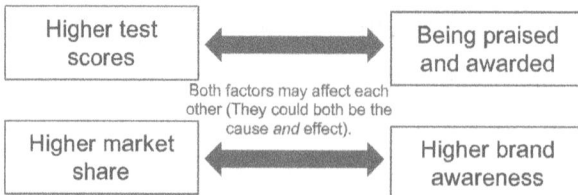

| Higher test scores | | Being praised and awarded |

Both factors may affect each other (They could both be the cause *and* effect).

| Higher market share | | Higher brand awareness |

7. Believing That There Is Only One Cause

Figure 4-15 illustrates how you might make a quick assumption that the sales revenue was high due to low pricing, disregarding other possible reasons such as the quality of your company's products and services, or brand strength.

Fig. 4-15 Are you forgetting any other factors?

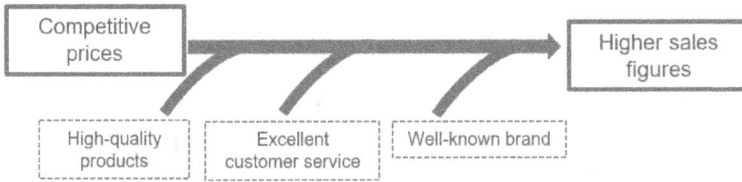

The scope of data can affect your conclusion.

As mentioned in Chapter 1 (Data Collection Tip No.3: Think about the scope of data that suits your objective.), your conclusion may change significantly, depending on which scope of data is used.

Fig. 4-16 Why the scope of data matters

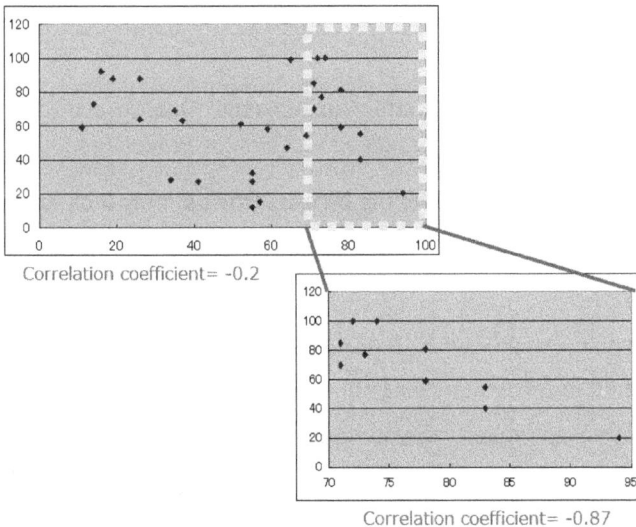

Correlation coefficient= -0.2

Correlation coefficient= -0.87

Figure 4-16 indicates two different results from the same data set (but using different scopes of data). In this case, "scope" means the "time-period" of the data used for analysis.

The correlation coefficient in the first scatter diagram is -0.2, while the second scatter diagram indicates -0.87. If this is a time-series case of the effectiveness of promotional activity x, you might conclude that:

- The effectiveness of promotional activity x is not correlated with elapsed time (first scatter diagram); or
- The effectiveness of promotional activity x is not correlated until a certain point in time; however, it starts decreasing after that point (second scatter diagram).

Which of the two conclusions above do you think is correct?

The answer depends on how you choose, or look at the scope of data.

This case applies not only to correlation analyses but to other analyses, too. Not everyone will get the same results even if they use the same data set.

Here are two key points that you should remember when you are selecting the scope of data for a correlation analysis:

- Use the scope of data that suits your objective. Don't use whatever data you have simply because you found it.
- Visualize data and look at the big picture. Don't simply look at the calculated correlation coefficient.

I visualize the relationship of data with scatter diagrams to confirm the above-mentioned points whenever I am checking important data. It helps you enhance the accuracy and quality of your analysis.

Outliers have a huge impact on your correlation coefficient.

Outliers which are even slightly off can have a huge impact on correlation. The correlation coefficient in Figure 4-5 is 0.95. If there were one strong outlier in the data (for whatever reason), the correlation coefficient of the entire data could now drop to 0.76 (**Figure 4-17**).

You should not rely only on the numerical value of the correlation coefficient because it does not necessarily explain the characteristics of the entire data set, which you could end up missing. To prevent this from happening, you can use a scatter diagram to look at the entire data set.

You should not omit the outlier automatically, though. Having an outlier is not always bad. Decide whether you should keep or omit the outlier in your data depending on your objective.

Fig. 4-17 Scatter diagram with an outlier

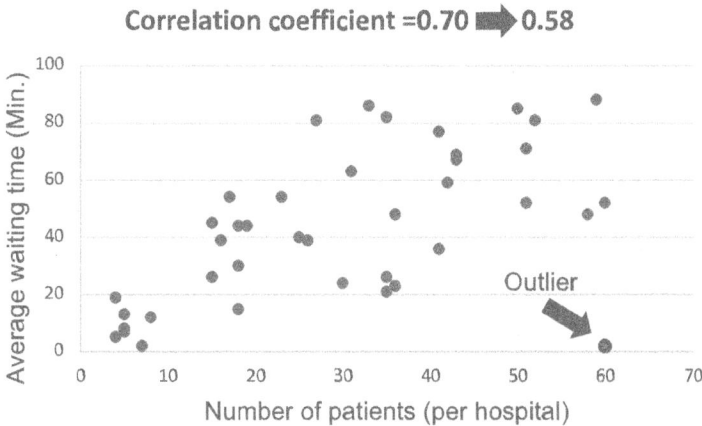

Correlation coefficient =0.70 ➡ 0.58

Factors Within Data

As I mentioned in Chapter 1, even if you have the same data, it can be decomposed into smaller factors, sometimes giving you different results.

Say, you are selling two types of audio equipment (high-end and standard products) and you analyzed data on the percentage increase in sales depending on how large of a discount was made. **Figure 4-18** is a scatter diagram in which both high-end and standard products are combined instead of counted separately. As you can see, the correlation coefficient is -0.14 and there is hardly any correlation between the data on the x-axis and the y-axis.

Fig. 4-18 Sales growth of audio devices (both high-end and standard products)

Correlation coefficient: -0.14

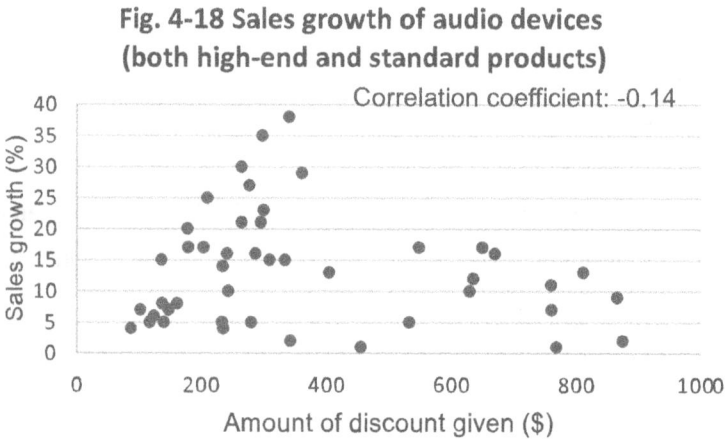

Did you draw a conclusion that offering a discount does not lead to an increase in sales? *Wait just a minute.*

Separate the high-end products from standard products.

In **Figure 4-19**, the data of high-end products are separated from those of standard products.

This time, there is a positive correlation in the scatter diagram for standard products. The correlation coefficient is 0.64, which is fairly high. Thus, you can see that customers who bought the standard products were more motivated to buy it when they were given discounts.

Fig. 4-19 Sales growth of audio devices (by grade)

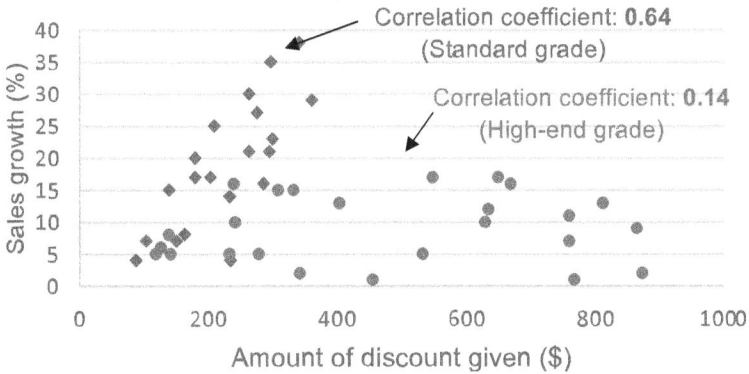

On the other hand, the correlation coefficient of the high-end product is 0.14, and there is hardly any correlation between the two data.

It is likely that customers who are already interested in purchasing such expensive products are not influenced by changes in pricing anyway. Therefore, price discounts are not effective.

As you can see, you may end up with incorrect analysis results if you combine and analyze data that has several different factors.

Realistically speaking, however, it is difficult for the person collecting or analyzing data to notice such factors, as it depends on one's knowledge and observation skills. You may end up using the original data as it is without noticing this problem.

To avoid this risk as much as possible, stop using data automatically and get used to checking whether the data can be decomposed into several factors. The attributes of time, region or customer (age, gender, income, industry, size of the organization, or preference) are some examples. Please be aware of the kinds of attributes (factors) that exist in your industry or career field.

You can also ask someone else to check your analysis.

I, too, don't always notice such factors and can't decompose data on my own all the time (especially when I had a tight schedule). Show your analysis results of the entire data to someone who has more knowledge and experience than you. He/she may give you an opinion or ask you a question if your analysis doesn't make sense. You might be able to see the data from new perspectives and further decompose the data to do a more detailed analysis.

That is an important lesson that I learned when I collected data, and it prevents me from running out of time after analyzing.

Think logically. What is the most effective method?

When you are trying to select the most reasonable option, do not rely on short-sighted ideas such as using the same exact strategy as that of the previous year, or that of a competitor. Also, don't rely solely on inspiration and plan logically. Otherwise, you will have a risky outcome.

If you want to use correlation at work, the most effective strategy is to look for something that is closely tied to the objective.

Say, you conducted an employee satisfaction survey to grasp the current mindset of employees. The survey included 30 questions like "whether the employees are getting enough paid leave." Employees answered each question on a scale from 1 to 5, which stood for the achievement rate. The percentage of employees who answered 5 ("strongly agree," or "well-achieved") or 4 ("somewhat agree," or "achieved to some degree") is shown on the y-axis. The correlation coefficient with the employee satisfaction score (1 to 5), is shown on the x-axis (**Figure 4-20**).

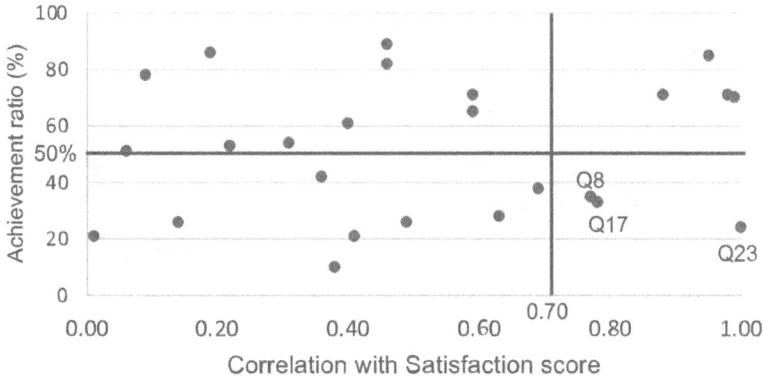

Fig. 4-20 Application example (Customer satisfaction survey)

In Figure 4-20, the small rectangular area in the bottom right corner shows the items that were strongly correlated with employee satisfaction but were not achieved (Questions 8, 17 and 23). The threshold depends on the analysis, but I set the threshold for the correlation coefficient to 0.7 and the achievement rate to 50% for this data set. It is clear from this scatter diagram that the items in Questions 8, 17 and 23 need to be prioritized and tackled first. Thus, I was able to apply correlation to clarify the issues which needed immediate improvement. Solving these issues would result in achieving the objective (employee satisfaction).

Effective Sales Strategies

Let's go back to Alex's example. Alex needs to propose a plan for the most effective sales strategy within the budget limitations of the company. From the results of the correlation analysis, Alex decided to prioritize investment in online ads and discount coupons.

Like Alex, you can use your data analysis results to compare the options and narrow them down to those that are more appropriate from an objective point of view.

Promotional Strategy	Correlation coefficient
Online ads (time lag: one month)	0.88
Discount coupons	0.90
In-store events	0.36

In Alex's example, we analyzed three strategies, but in general, you will have a lot more options that you need to choose from.

The more options you have, the more they tend to intertwine with one another and there is a higher possibility of spurious correlation.

For instance, product popularity is affected by (associated with) pricing, packaging, function, brand, customer service and aftercare. Customer service, packaging and brand are correlated with one another, so it is difficult to analyze how each factor affects (correlates with) product popularity independently. Please note this when you are choosing data.

Online Ads and Discount Coupons

How effective are they in increasing sales?

People with keen observation skills may notice that:

- You can use correlation to show the relationship between two data sets.
- This relationship can be shown with numbers.
- In Alex's case, the question is whether spending $10,000 on online ads would generate more profit than if the same amount is spent on discount coupons (or vice versa).

If you are in charge of the budget, once you answer this question, you will understand what to spend funds on.

I will discuss this further in the next chapter.

Alex decided that online ads and discount coupons were going to be his two promotional strategies to increase sales.

Alex: "I never thought about the time lag between the release of ads and the actual sales!"

Boss: "Yes, you need to consider what might happen in reality in addition to the data itself. Now that you have effective strategies to generate sales, make sure that sales exceeds expenses. Don't forget to do a cost-effectiveness analysis, which is important in management."

COLUMN: CALCULATING THE CORRELATION COEFFI-CIENT OF MORE THAN THREE DATA SETS

In this chapter, I showed you how to use Excel's CORREL function. This is a very useful tool that can analyze two data sets within seconds, so you will not waste time or energy. Try it whenever you may think it could be useful.

In many cases, though, there are more than two related data sets (e.g. sales data of a certain product, or employee satisfaction surveys consisting of multiple questions).

If there are ten types of data and you try to pair two data sets for analysis, there will be a total of forty-five different combinations, which can be a little overwhelming, even if each analysis only takes a few seconds.

In such cases, you can use the following Excel function to save time.

First, enable the Analysis ToolPak add-in in Excel. Select "Data Analysis." (The next steps depend on the version of Excel that you are using.)

From "Analysis Tools," select "Correlation." (**Figure 4-21**)

This will take you to the "Correlation" dialog box shown in **Figure 4-22**. Select the data range in "Input Range," and select the cell in which you want to display the result in "Output Range."

Fig. 4-21 Selecting "Correlation"

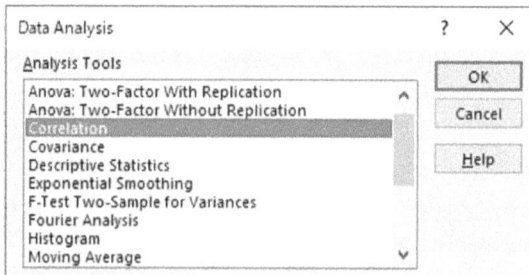

Fig. 4-22

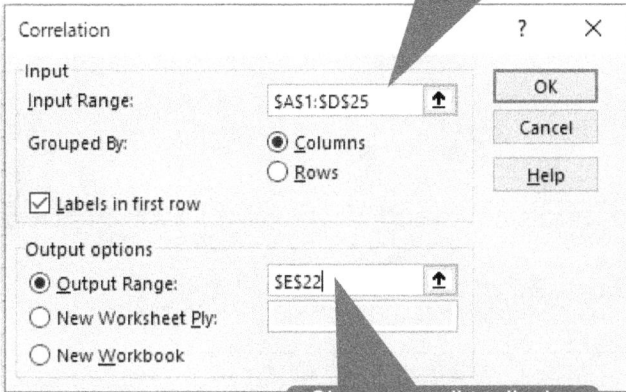

Let's use the Happy Planet Index (HPI) as an example. This is an index of wellbeing introduced by a UK-based think tank called the New Economics Foundation (NEF) (http://happyplanetindex.org).

The website collects and publishes an index relating to wellbeing in each country. Let's pick five types of data and look at the correlation between each of them: life expectancy, wellbeing, population, GDP/capita (economic indicator) and governance ranking.

Using the "Correlation" function mentioned above, the data sets of 150 countries were analyzed (See **Figure 4-23**).
The correlation coefficient for each combination within the five types of data is listed.

When identical data is compared, there is a perfect correlation, so the correlation coefficient is 1.

Fig. 4-23 Correlation Matrix for Wellbeing Indicators

	Life Expectancy (0-10)	Wellbeing (0-10)	Population	GDP/ Capita	Governance Ranking (1-highest)
Life Expectancy (0-10)	1				
Wellbeing (0-10)	0.71	1			
Population	0.00	-0.03	1		
GDP/ Capita	0.66	0.70	-0.07	1	
Governance Ranking (1-highest)	-0.67	-0.63	0.06	-0.75	1

Let's focus on correlation coefficients over 0.70.

Combinations	Correlation Coefficient	Notes
Life Expectancy & Wellbeing	0.71	Longevity is one of the values of happiness.
Wellbeing & GDP/Capita	0.70	Despite the saying that "money can't buy happiness," money seems to be quite important.
GDP/Capita & Governance	-0.75	The correlation coefficient is negative, because the higher the governance rank (the lower the number), the more effective governance is. This shows that wealthy countries have effective governance.

This result coincides with general views. It is clear that the size of the population is hardly related to other indicators.

There is a lot more information that you can obtain from this data. Please think about it.

Chapter 5

Setting the Target Value to Reach Your Goal

—Assess the plan and its profitability with regression analysis.

How much money needs to be spent to reach the goal?

Alex: "Correlation is so useful! Our sales team assumed that in-store events were effective in boosting sales and spent so much money on them, but no one actually checked how effective they were. I did a correlation analysis to find out the strength of the relationship between two data sets. Now I know how to use numbers to visualize information and fact-check such assumptions."

Boss: "That's fantastic! Correlation is very useful as long as you use it correctly."
"Ok, now it's time to finalize the business plan. We estimated the size of the market, looked into the risks and checked which promotion was the most effective. So, Alex... Do you understand what you need to say to get an approval? If you were one of the directors, what would be the key factors in approving the plan? That is the most important question. Are you prepared with an answer?"

Alex: "Not yet...Although I collected a lot of information, I still have no idea how to draw a conclusion."

Boss: "Ok. There's nothing wrong with your data collection and analysis of information. You just need a different approach. You've been collecting and adding useful bits of information each time you noticed something was missing. But what's actually important is <u>to think of the key factors, or conditions that help you get an approval, and to ask yourself what you need to meet those conditions. You have to change your perspective.</u>"
"Remember the 'hypothesis approach'? Since it was your first time learning analysis, I showed you how to keep adding new information each time you noticed the missing bits...but you know what? It's actually more effective and efficient to come up with a conclusion (what you want to say) and then collect information that supports your conclusion. Please use this method next time, and don't forget the 'hypothesis approach.'"

Alex: "Ah, yes. I learned so many analysis methods that I almost forgot about the 'hypothesis approach.'"

Boss: "So...do you have a conclusion that would convince the board?"

Alex: "Well...If I were one of the directors, I would want to know what we need in the first year to achieve the mid-term goals for the first five years."

Boss: "Exactly. It's unclear how much promotion—you chose online ads and discount coupons—is enough to achieve the goal. The board would not give the go-ahead unless you have this information."

Alex: "You're right. <u>If I can determine the promotional budget to generate more sales and reach the goal, I can prove that our company can enter this market successfully.</u>"

Boss: "Exactly. You just need to explain that with numbers and statistical analysis. You're almost there. You've got this!"

The result of your regression analysis supports the plan from an objective viewpoint.

To successfully enter the market in Country X, Alex set the mid-term goal: in five years, the company will increase sales by twofold from the initial sales (90,000 vacuum cleaners). Alex needs to figure out how much money needs to be spent in promotions to achieve this goal, or there is no way to check whether he has a good business plan. The plan is useless if the company cannot achieve the goal within its budget limitations.

How much money needs to be spent, then? To answer this question, you must first identify the factors that affect sales, and the magnitude of that effect.

Correlation analysis (see previous chapter) is an analysis method that helps you identify those factors that affect sales, by looking at the strength of their relationship with sales.

Correlation analysis comes in handy, as it is simple and easy to obtain the analysis results. On the other hand, you can find the strength of the relationship of two data sets, but not the size, or numerical value describing the relationship **(quantitative relation)**.

Quantitative relation is not a cause and effect relationship, but it uses numerical equations to describe the relationship between two data sets.

How do we describe this relationship with an equation?

As mentioned previously, correlation measures linear (proportional) relationships. As you have learned in school, the proportional relationship between the data sets X and Y is generally calculated with the following equation:

y = mx + b (m and b are constants)

You can find out the relationship between x and y once you know the values of m and b. In other words, you will understand how much x, or input (e.g. expenditures, or the number of staff, etc.), is necessary for y, or the expected output (e.g. sales, number of customers who come to the stores, etc.).

This numerical relationship between the correlated data sets x and y can be analyzed by **regression analysis**.

Estimate the amount of expenditures that will boost the effectiveness of the promotion.

In what kind of situation should the regression analysis be used to find the quantitative relationship, or equation, between data sets x and y?

For instance, if you know the quantitative relationship between sales and the expenditures for advertising and promotion, you can make this estimate:

"We need to spend $1,000 in advertising and promotion to boost sales by another $10,000."

Also, if you know the quantitative relationship between the temperature and the number of tourists at a destination, you can say:

"According to the weather forecast, the temperature for this coming weekend is going to be around 59°F (15°C), so the estimated number of tourist arrivals for this weekend is 500."

In both cases, you are estimating (calculating) the value of one data set by using information from another data set that you already have.

In regression analysis, the difference in units and size of numerical values in the two data sets do not matter (This is similar to the characteristics of correlation analysis). Thus, this analysis can be applied in many ways.

In Alex's case, regression analysis can be used to find out how much x, or input (e.g. expenditures, the number of staff, etc.) is necessary to achieve y, or the target sales in the business plan.

The plan may not be approved if the estimated expenditures or the number of staff go over the budget. On the other hand, it is likely to be approved if the expected output (e.g. sales and profit) exceeds the budget in the plan.

Either way, Alex needs to show the necessary expenditures in order for the board to make its decision.

> **The regression equation indicates the relationship between two data sets.**

The purpose of regression analysis is to calculate and determine the constants m and b and complete the equation y=mx+b (**regression equation**), which describes the relationship between the two data sets x and y.

Please note, however, that <u>the data sets need to be correlated</u>. If you use two data sets that are not correlated to form an equation showing the relationship of the data sets, that equation is not reliable.

This means that you must do a correlation analysis to confirm the correlation of the two data sets (Remember the good rule of thumb: the correlation coefficient should be **at least 0.7**.) before getting into regression analysis.

I'll show you an example using Excel.

Start with a scatter diagram.

In my correlation analysis in Chapter 4, I used scatter diagrams to visualize data instead of relying solely on the correlation coefficient. This way, I could find out the characteristics of data and how outliers affect the whole data set. This information could only be detected visually from scatter diagrams.

Scatter diagrams are also useful for regression analysis.

To do a regression analysis, start drawing a scatter diagram. The linear function that most closely represents the whole data set is the regression equation.

What does "closely represent" mean? Once you are able to answer this question, you will have mastered regression analysis.

What does "closely represent" and "R-squared" mean?

Figure 5-1 is a scatter diagram showing the relationship of sales and expenditures for the distribution of discount coupons. A straight line is drawn through the middle of the whole data set. Unless the above-mentioned sales and expenditures are perfectly correlated, the data will not form a straight line. Some data will fall outside of the line.

Fig. 5-1 How a regression line is identified

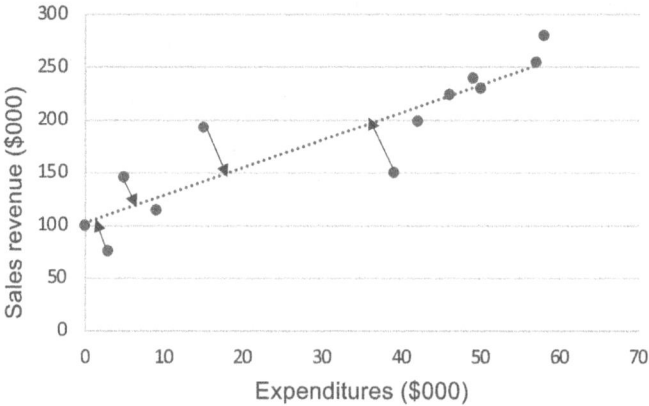

If you want to describe the trend of the data with a line, you can only draw a line which has the least amount of outliers and which most closely represents the relationship of the data sets.

The "closest" line is the **regression equation** that you want to form.

In analysis, the regression equation is calculated by drawing a line that best fits the data, with the smallest overall distance between the line and the plotted data points.

Even if the distance from the data points is the smallest, the regression equation will not accurately represent the trend in data if the equation and each data point have a large disparity. **R-squared**, or **R2**, is an indicator showing how accurately the regression equation represents the actual data, i.e., whether the total distance between the data points and the regression line is reasonable.

To understand how R-squared works, let's think again about what the distance between the data points and the regression line means.

Theoretically, the best distance is zero, meaning that all data points lie on the regression line (there is no distance between the data points and the regression line).

In Chapter 4, this is described as a **perfect correlation**. The correlation (proportional relationship) weakens gradually as each data point moves away from the line.

This theory can be applied to regression analysis and R-squared as well.

Fig. 5-2 Linear relationship, Correlation and R-squared

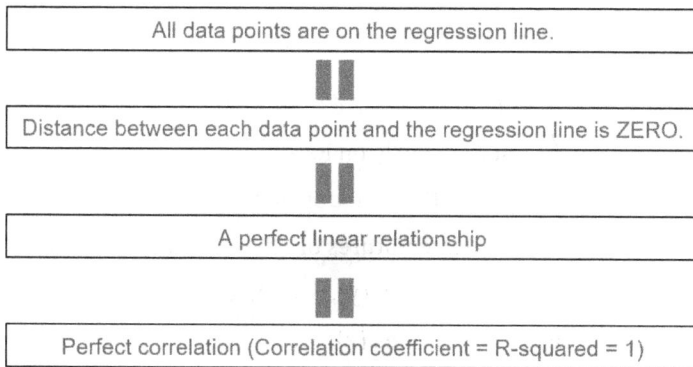

All data points are on the regression line.

Distance between each data point and the regression line is ZERO.

A perfect linear relationship

Perfect correlation (Correlation coefficient = R-squared = 1)

The value of R-squared is 1 when all data points lie on the regression line and the line perfectly represents the whole data set. The value decreases as each data point shifts away from the line, finally becoming 0. Unlike the correlation coefficient, however, there are no negative values in R-squared.

Figure 5-3 shows the regression line, regression equation and R-squared derived from a scatter diagram. The correlation coefficient of the data set is 0.90.

Fig. 5-3 Regression line and R-squared on a scatter diagram

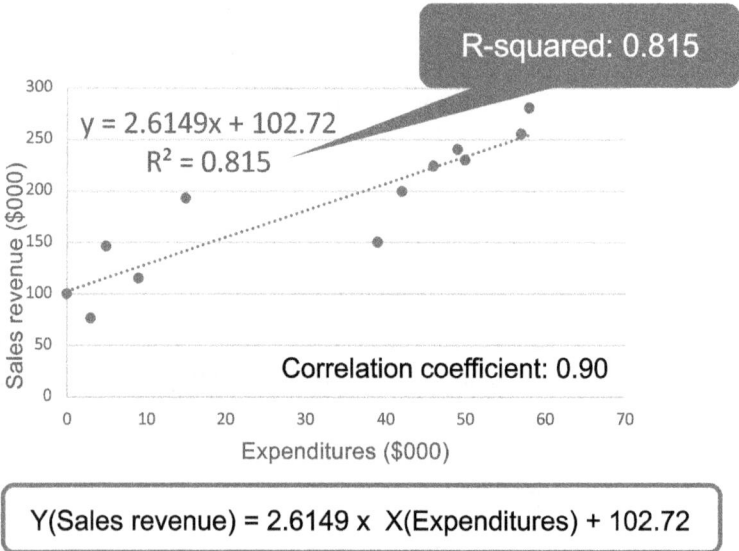

Y(Sales revenue) = 2.6149 x X(Expenditures) + 102.72

The regression equation is y = 2.6149x + 102.72 and R-squared is 0.815 (They can be calculated simultaneously on Excel).

Say, there is a quantitative relationship in which sales is boosted by $27,500 with each increase in expenditures on discount coupons of $10,000.

If your sales target is $200,000 (y), you can calculate the amount of expenditures necessary for discount coupons (x).

y = 2.6149x + 102.72

200 (in $000s) = 2.6149x + 102.72

x ≒ 37.2 (in $000s)

This means that at least $37,200 should be spent on discount coupons to reach your sales target.

The threshold of R-squared is 0.5.

We should not assess whether our analysis results are reasonable based on our personal opinions. Unfortunately, though, there is no standard value of R-squared that determines whether the regression equation is appropriate (The same thing can be said with the correlation coefficient).

Look at Figure 5-3 again. Are there any hints in this diagram on how to set a threshold value of R-squared?

Compare the values of the correlation coefficient and R-squared. Also, what does "squared" mean in R-squared?

You may have noticed that **R-squared is the square of the correlation coefficient.** Both the correlation coefficient and R-squared show the disparity between the data points and the line, and they are obviously closely related to each other. Because R-squared is a square value, it always turns out positive whether the correlation coefficient is a positive or negative value.

What, then, is the threshold value of R-squared that we can rely on? As mentioned previously, in my experience, 0.7 has been a reliable threshold value of the correlation coefficient. Using this number, R-squared should be 0.49 (= 0.7×0.7). I believe that 0.5 is a reliable value, and it should be at least 0.5. In Figure 5-3, R-squared is 0.82 and it surpasses the threshold.

Using Excel for Regression Analysis

I will show you how to use Excel for regression analysis. Let's use the scatter diagram in Figure 5-3 again.

1. Right-click a data point on the scatter diagram. Any point is fine.
2. As you can see in the bottom right corner of Figure 5-4, select "Add Trendline."
3. Select "Linear" (See Figure 5-5. The format varies depending on the version of your Excel).
4. Select "Display Equation on chart" and "Display R-squared value on chart," and then close. The regression equation and the R-squared value will be shown automatically on the scatter diagram.

Fig. 5-4 Regression analysis with Excel

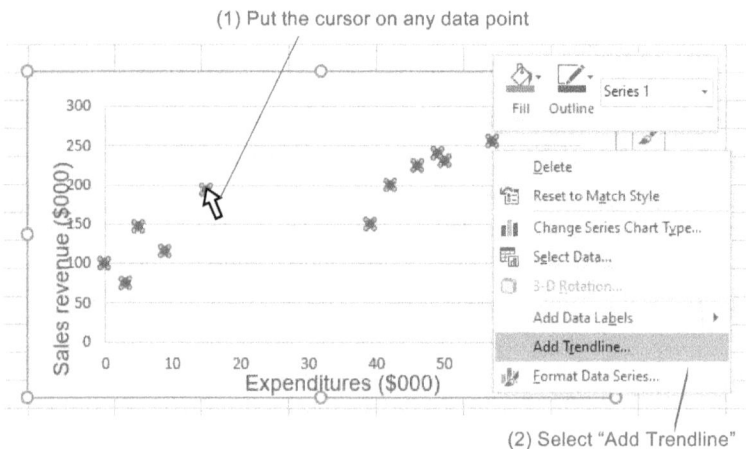

As you can see, it is very simple and easy to do regression analysis with Excel. You can quickly complete the following procedures and repeat trial and error using a variety of data:

Preparation of data → Correlation analysis → Make a scatter diagram → Regression analysis

Fig. 5-5 Regression analysis with Excel

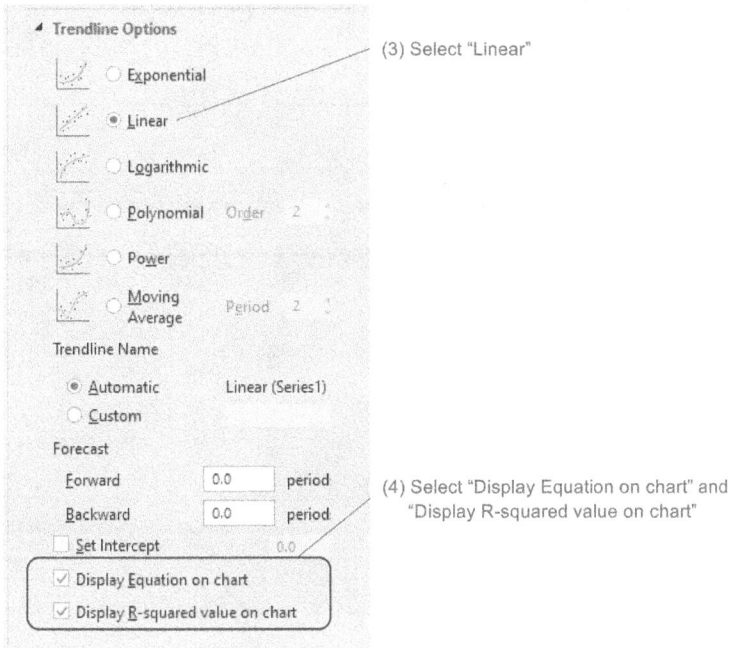

Trendline Options

○ Exponential

● Linear ————————— (3) Select "Linear"

○ Logarithmic

○ Polynomial   Order   2

○ Power

○ Moving
   Average   Period   2

Trendline Name

● Automatic   Linear (Series1)
○ Custom

Forecast

Forward   0.0   period   (4) Select "Display Equation on chart" and
                             "Display R-squared value on chart"
Backward   0.0   period

☐ Set Intercept   0.0

☑ Display Equation on chart
☑ Display R-squared value on chart

The condition for regression analysis is that the two data sets need to be correlated to a certain extent. If you find out that a strong correlation does not exist, you should stop there.

As you can see from the different "Trendline Options," or functions in Figure 5-5, regression analysis can also be used in cases where there is no proportional (linear) relationship. Although you could try using different functions and pick the most accurate one, I would still pick a linear function. It is the most convincing relationship and easy to explain to people unfamiliar with statistical analysis.

Try using logarithms and exponentials. You may end up having an accurate analysis that no one else understands. You may appear sophisticated, but a great majority of people would not understand what you are saying, no matter how hard you try (unless you are at an academic conference). I have learned this the hard way!

How well-designed is your plan? Is it profitable?

Which promotional strategy is more effective?

Alex did a regression analysis on the relationship between expenditures and sales revenue for online ads and discount coupons (See Figures 5-6 and 5-7).

Fig. 5-6 Expenditure on Online Ads and Sales

Online Ads

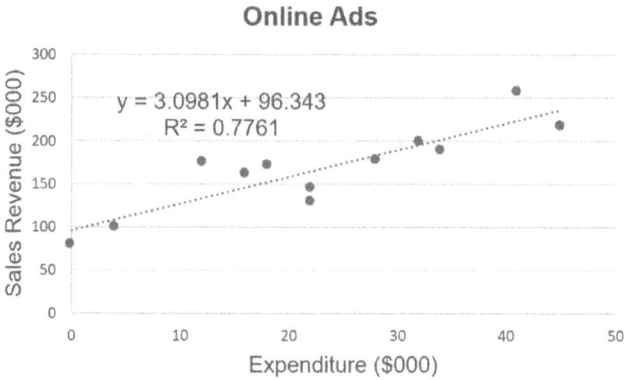

$y = 3.0981x + 96.343$
$R^2 = 0.7761$

Fig. 5-7 Expenditure on Discount Coupons and Sales

Discount Coupons

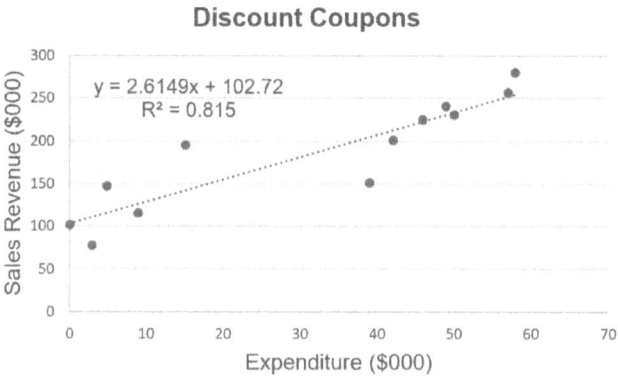

$y = 2.6149x + 102.72$
$R^2 = 0.815$

Regression equation: y = mx + b

Online ads:

y = 3.0981x + 96.343

Sales (in $000s) = 3.0981 × Expenditures (in $000s) + 96.343

Discount coupons:

y = 2.6149x + 102.72

Sales revenue (in $000s) = 2.6149 × Expenditures (in $000s) + 102.72

Regression equations are useful when you want to compare two promotional strategies and find out which one is more effective, or when you want to know the amount of expenditures necessary when you decide to rely on a single strategy.

You can find out which promotion is more effective by checking how much of an increase there is in sales revenue with every $1,000 increase in promotional expenditures. This is described by the constant "m" (slope) in the regression equation. The slopes for online ads and discount coupons are 3.0981 and 2.6149, respectively. Say, you spend $1,000 each.

With online ads, the increase in sales revenue is:

Sales revenue (in $000s) = 3.0981 × 1 ($000s) + 96.343 =99.4411

With discount coupons, the increase in sales revenue is:

Sales revenue (in $000s) = 2.6149 × 1 ($000s) + 102.72 =105.3349

105.3349 - 99.4411 = 5.8938 ($000s)

Discount coupons are more effective than online ads in boosting sales revenue by $5,893.80 when $1,000 is spent on each strategy.

Let's also look at R-squared and the correlation coefficient explained in Chapter 4.

	Slope	Correlation coefficient	R-squared
Online ads	3.0981	0.88	0.78
Discount coupons	2.6149	0.90	0.82

The correlation coefficient shows that online ads have a weaker correlation with sales revenue than discount coupons. Therefore, <u>the size of correlation and the size of the slope (effectiveness of the strategy) are unrelated.</u>

It is not easy to compare a data set with a steeper slope and a weaker correlation (online ads) and another data set with a gradual slope and a stronger correlation (discount coupons). If a data point is right on the regression line, it means that online ads are very impactful in generating sales revenue. However, there is more risk of outliers; an increase in expenditures in online ads would not necessarily lead to a boost in sales revenue. On the other hand, discount coupons have a higher chance in increasing sales revenue, but the impact, or the effectiveness, is not as large as with online ads. When choosing between a strategy that is more effective (larger impact) and another one that has a higher chance, there is no straightforward answer as to which choice would be better.

In Alex's example, the correlation coefficient is pretty high in both online ads and discount coupons. (Any value equal to or greater than 0.7 is a "pass" in my opinion. I do not necessarily think that one correlation coefficient is better than the other just because it is a slightly larger value.)

We have only considered cases where only one strategy is implemented at a time. If both strategies are implemented simultaneously at the same place (in the same market), perhaps it is better to use a **multiple regression analysis** (see column at the end of this chapter) instead of the regression equation. Several types of data can be analyzed with multiple regression analyses.

How to Utilize the Regression Equation

1. Expected Annual Expenditures on Online Ads

How, then, can Alex use the regression equation? Say, the target annual sales revenue after entering the new market is $38 million. With the data of Country Y, the regression equation was an analysis of a limited region. If the trade area of Country X is five times as large as that of Country Y, then the target annual sales revenue in Country X, boosted by online ads, is described by the equation below.

S = Target annual sales revenue in Country X = 38,000 (in $000s)
M = monthly expenditures in Country Y (in $000s)
A = the expected annual expenditures in Country X (in $000s)
Market size of trade area in Country X = 5
Months = 12

S = 38,000 (in $000s) = {3.0981M + 96.343} $\times$ 5 $\times$ 12
38,000 $\div$ 60 = 3.0981M + 96.343
M $\fallingdotseq$ 173

A = M $\times$ 5 $\times$ 12 $\fallingdotseq$ 10,380
A $\div$ S = 10,380 $\div$ 38,000 $\fallingdotseq$ 0.27

Therefore, monthly expenditures in Country Y are around $170,000, and the **expected annual expenditures on online ads** in Country X are around **$10 million**. This is about 27% of target sales revenue.

2. Expected Annual Expenditures on Discount Coupons

Similarly, the target annual sales revenue in Country X, boosted by discount coupons, is described by the equation below.

38,000 (in \$000s) = {2.6149M + 102.72}$\times$5$\times$12

38,000 $\div$ 60 = 2.6149M + 102.72

M $\fallingdotseq$ 203

A = M$\times$5$\times$12= 12,180

A $\div$ S = 12,180 $\div$ 38,000 $\fallingdotseq$ 0.32

Therefore, monthly expenditures in Country Y are around \$200,000, and the **expected annual expenditures on discount coupons** in Country X are around **\$12 million**. This is about 32% of target sales revenue.

      If you implement both strategies (alternatively, etc.) then the expected annual expenditures should be between 10 and 12 million dollars.

      To enter the new market, it is essential for the management to decide whether the initial expenditures plan for the first year is reasonable. How to make this decision will vary depending on the type of product or industry. Also, are the expenditures under the budget in the first place?

      Regression analysis is a powerful tool to form equations and make projections based on data which can guide your decision making.

> ### Regression Analysis Tip No.1: Slopes show the effectiveness and efficiency of expenditures.
> *The Amount of Promotional Expenditures Necessary to Boost Sales Revenue*

Using regression analysis, you can find out the quantitative relationship between data sets X and Y by entering one data to calculate the other data. This can help you make forecasts or calculate the amount of X (expenditures, etc.) necessary to achieve Y (sales revenue, etc.).

In the next section, I will show you other ways to apply regression analysis.

The slope tells you the effectiveness and efficiency of the promotion expenditures.

Alex did a correlation analysis and a regression analysis to form the following regression equations:

Online ads:	Sales revenue (in $000s) = 3.0981 × Expenditures (in $000s) + 96.343
Discount coupons:	Sales revenue (in $000s) = 2.6149 × Expenditures (in $000s) + 102.72

In the regression equation $y = mx+b$, the slope (m) shows the rate of increase in y when x increases by one unit. When expenditures increase by one unit ($1,000), sales revenue increases by 3.0981 ($3,098.10) with online ads, and by 2.6149 ($2,614.90) with discount coupons.

In other words, the slope describes the efficiency of expenditures.

From a cost-effectiveness perspective, if you spend the same amount of money, online ads are more effective, leading to a larger boost in sales revenue than with discount coupons.

However, as I mentioned, there are other things to consider besides the size of the slope; please read the following points.

● Is the correlation too weak?

Even if the slope is steep, a weak correlation means that the possibility of a data point falling on the regression line is low. As I mentioned earlier, effectiveness and efficiency are not related to the values of the correlation coefficient and R-squared which describe the probability of a data point falling on the regression line.

● Is it realistic?

The regression line (proportional relationship) in regression analysis is a simplified version of reality.

In Alex's case, it is not realistic to rely on the analysis results and focus on spending money on online ads only. There should be a limit to how much sales revenue can be generated using one type of promotion; it is unlikely that there is an infinite effect of expenditures on sales revenue. It might be more realistic to implement both promotional strategies proportionally according to the ratio from the results of the regression analysis.

In real life, it is almost impossible to have a perfect linear relationship that keeps increasing infinitely. You need to take into account some common sense and the scope of your data, etc., to determine to what extent the results of the regression analysis can be used.

Regression Analysis Tip No.2: Identify the outcome unrelated to the factor.
Results That Can Be Achieved Without the Promotions

Let's look at the **intercept (b)** in the regression equation y=mx+b. The intercept is the value of data y when data x is zero. In Alex's example, the intercept is the expected sales revenue even when promotional strategies have zero effect on sales revenue (between $96,343 and $102,720). If the target sales revenue is under this amount (less than the intercept), you shouldn't spend any money on the promotion.

So, in what kind of situation is the intercept useful?

In reality, companies would not just wait for customers to buy their products without implementing any strategies, so there is no way of knowing what the sales revenue would be like if no promotional strategies had been implemented. However, we can calculate its theoretical value by using the intercept in the regression analysis.

Say, a certain amount of money was spent on promotion, and the outcome in sales revenue was $120,000. How much of that amount was boosted by the promotion? You can find this out by subtracting the value of the intercept (the sales revenue when no promotion is implemented):

$120,000 - $102,720 = **$17,280**

Thus, $17,280 is the amount of sales revenue boosted by the promotion. Regression analyses are a great tool in running this type of simulation.

Regression Analysis Tip No.3: Decompose data and find more detailed facts.

Determining Your Hours of Operation

When you're opening a new store, you need to decide its business hours.

If you have a hypothesis that sales revenue will increase when business hours are longer, you can test this hypothesis with the past sales revenue of several other existing stores, by checking the correlation between their business hours and sales revenue.

Say, you collected data from 45 different stores, and found that the correlation coefficient between business hours and sales revenue was 0.81. Figure 5-8 is a scatter diagram with the results of a regression analysis.

The correlation coefficient is high enough (above the threshold value (0.70)).

You can stop the analysis here but you may find more details if you dig a step further.

Fig. 5-8 A regression analysis result: "Revenue vs Business hours"

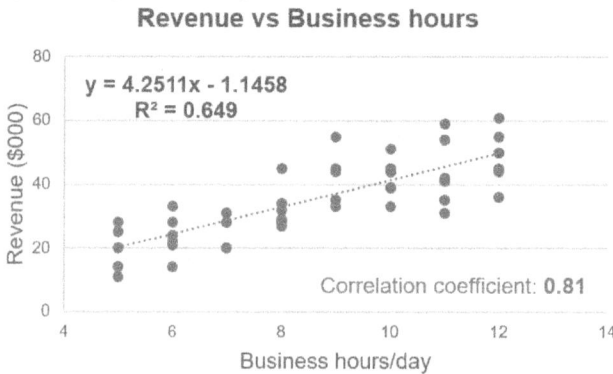

One solution is to decompose the data (see Chapter 1).

Say, you noticed that some stores were older than the other stores (Whether you notice this depends upon your instincts. You will gain a wider perspective and your instinct will become shrewder as your experience increases). Perhaps you would come up with a hypothesis that customers act differently depending on how old and well-established a store is.

Figure 5-9 shows the results of regression analyses of stores that opened less than a year ago, those that have been operating for one to five years, and those that have existed for five years or longer.

In all three categories, there was a correlation between business hours and sales revenue. Look at the value of m (slope) of the regression equations. The newer the store, the larger (steeper) the slope.

This means that the newer the stores, the more that sales revenue are generated when business hours are extended for another hour.

It may be premature to form a conclusion from this data that "newer stores get more attention, thus they generate more sales revenue when business hours are extended," but it might be a good estimate.

Either way, the difference in the regression analysis in Figures 5-8 and 5-9 (when the number of years of establishment is less than a year) is significant (slopes 4.2511 and 6.3875).

By getting more creative and decomposing the data, you may be able to obtain a more accurate analysis result.

Compare **Figures 5-9 and 5-10**. You will find more valuable information in Fig. 5-10.

Fig. 5-9 Results by the number of years since establishment

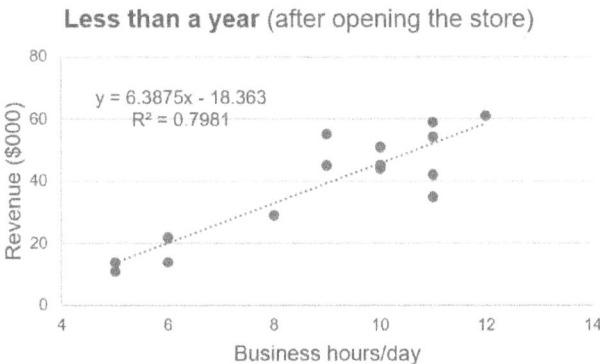

Less than a year (after opening the store)

$y = 6.3875x - 18.363$
$R^2 = 0.7981$

One to five years (after opening the store)

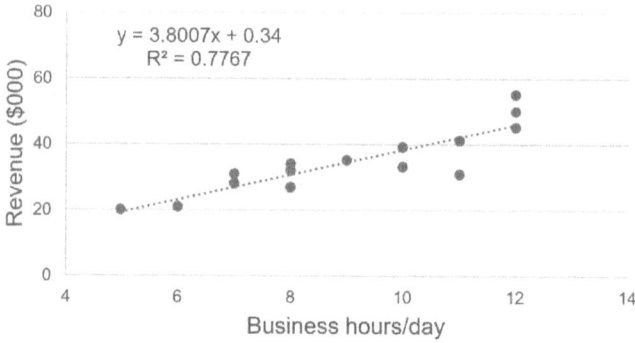

$y = 3.8007x + 0.34$
$R^2 = 0.7767$

Revenue ($000)

Business hours/day

Five years or more (after opening the store)

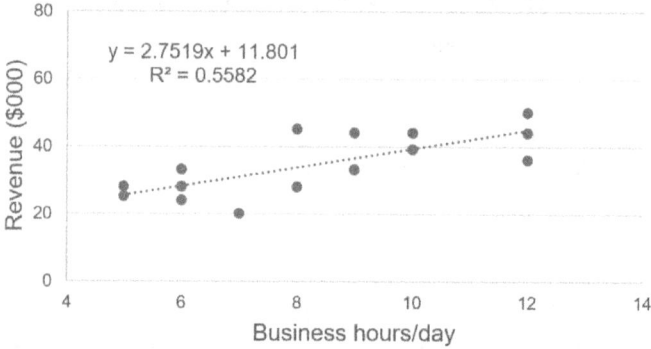

$y = 2.7519x + 11.801$
$R^2 = 0.5582$

Revenue ($000)

Business hours/day

Fig. 5-10 Breaking down the data makes a difference

Revenue vs Business hours

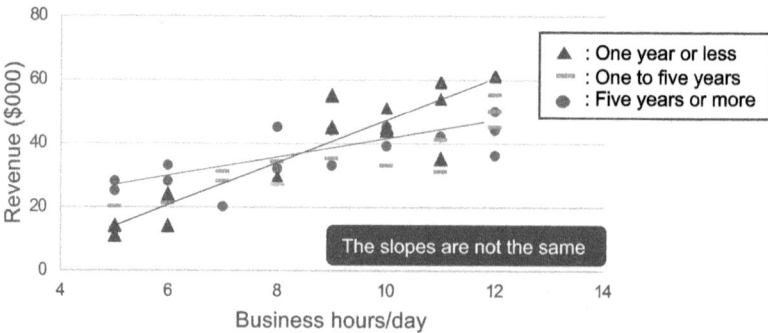

Revenue ($000)

▲ : One year or less
— : One to five years
● : Five years or more

The slopes are not the same

Business hours/day

Past conditions do not always apply to the future.

The regression equation is derived from regression analysis. If you have one data, then the other data can be calculated automatically and theoretically to make future forecasts. The forecast is based on what occurred in the past (data), with the assumption that the same conditions should continue to apply in the future.

"Wait a minute... is this really true?"

If you have this doubt, you have good instincts. There is a limit to regression analysis (and most other statistical and data analysis).

Remember, even if you are trying to predict the future, you are still basing it on past data. Don't get overconfident with your analysis results without taking into account this principle and the limit of regression analysis, because the results could be misleading.

For example, if the industry is evolving rapidly, is it ok to make business decisions from regression equations based on past data? What if the market is very different from what it used to be when you collected your data? Should this fact be ignored while you are analyzing the data?

Please remember that regression analysis simplifies past data and perceives information as fixed, instead of changing.

Critical thinking skills affect the accuracy and quality of an analysis result. To the experienced analyst, your analysis may look inexperienced and lose its credibility unless you take the conditions and limitations of analysis into account.

A critical mindset is more crucial than ever as society and ways of doing business change rapidly.

Regression Analysis Tip No.4: Organizational Planning and KPI

In entering a new market, you should not only forecast sales revenue but also prepare a system that supports your business. Your company may establish a new regional office, or simply add a new branch within the headquarters.

Whether your company is entering a new market or not, you may have a hard time deciding the correct number of employees, or setting the **Key Performance Indicator (KPI)**, which is a set of performance measurements that demonstrate how effectively an organization is at achieving key objectives. Many businesses simply follow established precedents or the consensus of management without giving them a second thought.

In these situations, correlation and regression analyses come in handy.

Say, you interviewed each division or department manager about their criteria, or indicator in deciding the number of employees to be hired.

They might give you the following answers:

- **Human Resources:** "We base our decision on the number of employees throughout the whole company."
- **Sales:** "We base our decision on sales figures, the number of customers, the number of stores, and the product lineup."
- **Marketing:** "We base our decision on the number of categories of products, and the number of languages used in promoting them."
- **Accounting:** "We base our decision on the number of transactions and the number of offices overseas."

If you find a correlation between an indicator and the numbers of employees in each department or division, that would help you determine the number of employees to hire from an objective viewpoint. You can calculate the number of employees to be hired from the relationship between the indicator and the number of employees derived from regression analysis.

Fig. 5-11 Identify the companies with an efficient HR department

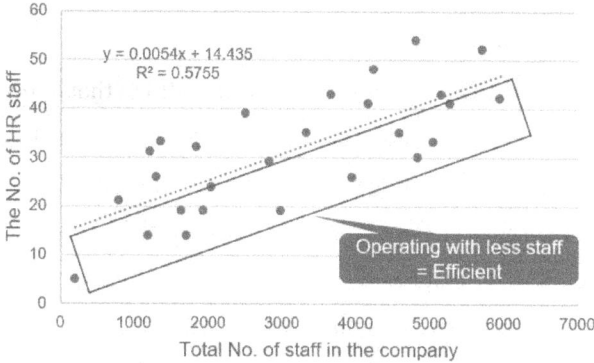

Figure **5-11** is the result of a regression analysis from a scatter diagram with the number of employees in the Human Resources Department and the office as a whole, in twenty different locations (domestic and overseas, including subsidiaries). As you can see, there is a correlation in the data. The regression equation shows that, the number of employees typically necessary in the Human Resources Department is around 0.7 per every 100 employees in the office. However, this is not necessarily the right answer. Some offices may want to pare down the number of employees to make it more efficient, rather than simply relying on existing data.

In Figure 5-11, the data points under the regression line show the offices which hired a smaller number of employees. You could select one of these offices and learn how they managed to operate their business more efficiently than the other offices.

Regarding the KPI for each department, try the following procedures as an application of what you have learned from this book:

1. What is the indicator for the performance goal of that department? (In sales, it might be the number of new customers, the ratio of successful sales, the ratio of repeated purchases, etc.)

2. What is the indicator for the performance goal of the company/business (sales, profit, etc.)?

3. Select an indicator from No. 1 that is strongly correlated with No. 2 as the KPI of that department.

4. Use a regression analysis to calculate the target KPI of that department in relation to the goals of the company or business. (You can set the KPI to the ratio of repeated purchases, since it is strongly correlated with sales. If your ultimate goal is to boost sales by 10%, your KPI may need to be raised from 20% (current KPI) to 35%, for instance.)

5. Use correlation analyses to regularly check whether the activities of your department are related to the selected KPI. (If the ratio of repeated purchases is the KPI, check its correlation with activities such as calling, or sending direct mail and newsletters to existing customers. If there is no correlation, these activities don't contribute to repeated purchases, and thus you need to change your approach.)

Use as a goal for individuals.

You can also set individual KPIs and goals in the same way.

If there is a strong correlation between the number of customers entering the store and the success rate in sales, it is reasonable to set the number of customers as a goal for each individual in order to reach the ultimate goal of the department: to increase the success rate in sales. Using a regression analysis, you can calculate the number of customers theoretically needed to achieve your goal (e.g. a sales rate of 50%).

Not all departments (functions) will necessarily provide you with an indicator that is proportional (correlated) to how your business is doing. For instance, the number of employees in the Strategic Planning Department or the General Affairs Department may not be directly related to business performance and it might be hard to find such an indicator, if any. Perhaps it is more reasonable to think on a case-by-case basis, in accordance with the requirements of each department, considering past data or the data of competitors.

One way of determining KPI is to use correlation to pick the right indicator, then a regression analysis to determine the right numerical value.

Alex: "We should spend $10 million on online ads and $12 million on discount coupons. I just need a budget approval. It's good to have reliable numbers for decision making."

Boss: "Exactly. You can't just pick a random number for such an important business decision."

Alex is starting to feel more confident in preparing for the presentation.

COLUMN: SIMPLE AND MULTIPLE REGRESSION ANALYSIS

What we have been doing in this chapter is actually called **"simple regression analysis"**, which is different from **"multiple regression analysis"**. As I mentioned, simple regression analysis describes the relationship between two data sets (x and y). On the other hand, multiple regression analysis describes the relationship between y and at least two more data sets $(x_1, x_2, x_3...)$ with the equation below:

$$y = ax_1 + bx_2 + cx_3 + dx_4 + ... + e$$
("a", "b", "c", "d"... and "e" are constants.)

Here is an example:

$$y = 2.1\,x_1 + 3.5\,x_2 + 0.8\,x_3 + 1.6\,x_4 + 45.7$$

y: customer satisfaction score (on a scale from 0 to 100)

x_1: customer service score

x_2: brand indicator

x_3: price

x_4: variety of products

When doing a regression analysis, your objective is to find the value(s) of the constant(s) in the equation. In simple regression analysis, the constants were "m" and "b". There are more constants in a multiple regression analysis. In the example above, a=2.1, b=3.5, c=0.8, d=1.6, and e=45.7. (I just made up these numbers to illustrate an example.)

There is only one explanatory variable (data set x) in simple regression analysis, which is quite a simplified way of looking at the real world. Multiple regression analysis is used to understand a more complex situation.

Why, then, did I only use simple regression analysis throughout this chapter? Multiple regression analysis is much more difficult to understand, since there are multiple explanatory variables (data sets).

1. Scatter diagrams can no longer be used, since the relationship between the data sets is no longer two dimensional (the x and y axis) and becomes at least three dimensional. Therefore, the analysis procedures get very complicated. (In Excel, you can do multiple regression analysis by clicking the "Data Analysis" button and then selecting "Regression.")

2. Correlated data sets affect each other, making it difficult to analyze. You need to keep changing the data combinations until you meet some requirements for statistical analysis. You may not reach any answers.

3. You need a lot of knowledge to understand the results of a multiple regression analysis (Once you learn, it's not an issue). This means that you must share some background knowledge to the audience before explaining your analysis results.

I use multiple regression analyses in cases where simple regression analyses is so simple that the results obviously don't make any sense to me nor the audience, and multiple regression analyses might provide more accurate and convincing results, or in cases where the results of multiple regression analyses might easily meet some statistical requirements. Nevertheless, I rarely use them because of their complexity.

Chapter 6

Present Your Numerical Data with a Message

Showing data is not enough!

Alex estimated the expenditure necessary to enter the new market, and is now in the finalization process of the presentation.

Boss: "Now that we're done analyzing data, we need to focus on how to *present* the business plan to get the go-ahead."

Alex: "Yes, I have all the numbers. Now, I'll start preparing the presentation material."

Boss: "We don't have much time left. I'll give you some key takeaways about how to prepare the material. *Think carefully* during your preparation."

Alex: "What do you mean by *'think carefully'*? I have all the data I need. I thought I only had to put them together and make a presentation."

Boss: "That's not enough...You see, giving a presentation is like cooking."

Alex: "Cooking..?"

Boss: "Yes. In cooking, even if you start off with the same ingredients, the outcome—the appearance or taste of the dish—will be completely different depending on how you cook those ingredients. It's the same thing with giving a presentation. <u>Even if you have the same data, the outcome will be completely different depending on how you show the data.</u> It all depends on how good you are at showing it."

"It's actually very challenging to present data effectively instead of just organizing and listing the analysis results. You need to give it a lot of thought."

Alex: "I understand...well, sort of..."

Boss: "Get creative! This is your last chance to earn extra points on your final output. Now's a good time to show off your presentation skills and add value to your business plan."

Alex: "I see. Would you give me a few more hints?"

Boss: "Sure! There's no exact science to making a great presentation, but I'll give you some takeaways. The rest is up to your ideas and creativity. I'm counting on you!"

Analyzing and presenting are two different things.

Alex finished analyzing the data, and he is enjoying a sense of accomplishment. If Alex drops his guard too early, however, his analysis will go to waste.

. What are some key points to remember when you want your audience to understand your analysis results?

Analyzing and explaining the analysis results are two completely different tasks. Your objective, way of thinking, and technique necessary for each task is different.

As is often the case, the person analyzing the data may also be tasked with doing the presentation. This is not always an issue, but you need to remember to change your way of thinking drastically when you are doing each task.

That might sound too obvious, but you'll have a better understanding of the difference between the two tasks by looking at the following chart.

Fig. 6-1 Differences between "Data analysis" and "Presentation"

	Data analysis	Presentation (Message delivery)
Main objectives	- To find certain trends from the data - To forecast/simulate the future	- To share the conclusion/ message - Agreement, Acceptance
Main methods	- Statistics - Graphing	- Visualizing/illustrating - Speech, gesture etc.
Characteristics of the outputs	- The same results will be reached from the same data and methods	- Output may differ by person - No "correct" answer

In many cases, people waste too much time and energy solely on data analysis or they falsely believe that they have reached their goal when they complete their analysis. It is important to remember that preparing for a presentation is a whole different task from analysis (See **Figure 6-2**).

Fig. 6-2 Analysis Result and Conclusion

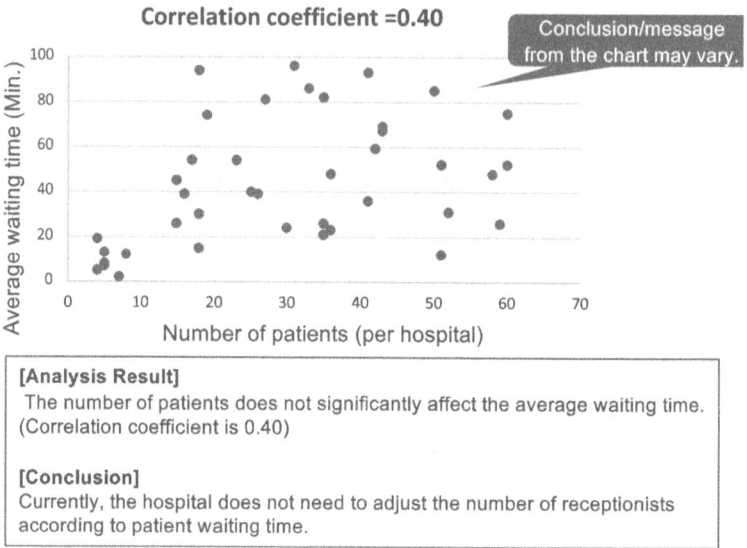

Correlation coefficient =0.40

Conclusion/message from the chart may vary.

[Analysis Result]
  The number of patients does not significantly affect the average waiting time.
  (Correlation coefficient is 0.40)

[Conclusion]
  Currently, the hospital does not need to adjust the number of receptionists according to patient waiting time.

Suppose that you show your audience the scatter diagram in Figure 6-2 as a conclusion and end your presentation at that point.

Some people may get the impression that: "So many patients wait over an hour before seeing the doctor. The hospital needs to increase the number of receptionists." Others may ask a lot of questions that are unanswered: "What does the correlation coefficient 0.40 mean? Does it mean that there is a relationship? What does this relationship have to do with the whole presentation?"

Thus, the interpretation of the analysis results varies widely depending on the audience.

What if you give a conclusion based on the analysis results instead? The "Analysis Result and Conclusion" (Figure 6-2) finishes the presentation with a clear message to the audience instead of letting them interpret the information freely. Conveying this kind of message is more challenging than you might think. You need to clarify the following points:

What do you want to tell your audience?

What do you want them to do with the analysis results?

Objective-based thinking, or going back to the objective to decide what action to take, is related to the hypothesis approach (see Preface). In other words, identifying your objective and intention is essential not only during data collection, but also during any other analysis procedures, including the finalization of the message you want to deliver to your audience. In the end, what you should be describing is not the analysis results themselves, but the intention, or *what you want to say* given the analysis results. (It is, of course, useful to show the analysis results as *supporting evidence* for your conclusion.)

Some analyses are intended for one's own reference or as preparation for other analyses, and not intended for an audience. Even in these situations, you still need to comprehend the analysis results based on your objective and summarize the key points.

Nevertheless, in most business situations, the objective of an analysis is to make your audience understand the analysis results or approve your proposal. You can't reach your goal unless you convince your audience. Your analysis results will only be meaningful if you convey your message effectively.

How to Convey Your Message Clearly

It is not easy to convey your message clearly. You need to use your head in many ways.

There is no correct answer, and if 100 people had the same analysis results, there would be 100 different ways to convey the message. There may be clear-cut answers to work procedures, but there are no clear answers for "how you should think and develop your ideas." However, here is some advice that may be useful.

Maintaining Objectivity

1. Don't try to explain the entire analysis.

The harder you work on your analysis and the more you achieve from it (especially when you achieve your anticipated analysis results), the more satisfied you may feel and you may want to share that accomplishment with your audience. However, your desire to show all of your "precious" analysis procedures and results to your audience may not be out of generosity, but in fact, it may be due to your conceit.

Take a step back and think whether the information is *necessary to the audience.*

At this point, you need to stop thinking like an analyst and switch your way of thinking to that of the speaker.

In Figure 6-2, suppose that you want to tell your audience that the waiting time does not change when the number of patients increases, and that it is unnecessary to change the number of receptionists (as long as the current waiting time is acceptable)In this case, you do not necessarily need to display a scatter diagram.

I am not saying that you should *never* show the scatter diagram. It can help convey the following information:

- The actual waiting time is between 18 and 100 minutes (The audience may think that 100 minutes is too long, which may start a new topic).
- The number of patients in the waiting room per hospital is constantly between 8 and 50, to which the audience may nod and say "Oh, I see," but it may not come as a shock.
- In addition to the correlation coefficient, a scatter diagram helps your audience understand data visually, which is more reassuring and convincing than explaining with words. The diagram shows that there is no particular trend in the data.

As I mentioned, none of this information is *necessary* in conveying the most important message to your audience or to help them understand it. If you include such nonessential information—depending on its size—it may distract your audience and your argument may lose its focus.

What is important is to <u>prioritize and rank information depending on whether or not it is essential</u> in conveying your message. My advice for you is to select any and all essential information based on your ranking and leave out any nonessential information as much as possible.

Some basic information may be obvious and easy to understand to the experienced analyst. For people who are being exposed to that kind of information for the first time, however, it's a lot to take in. Even the most intelligent people have a limit on how much information they can process and understand at a given time. Focusing on key points could help you achieve a win-win—you can convey your message clearly, and your audience can understand what you mean.

When you have already been dealing with a copious amount of information while performing an analysis, it may be difficult to notice how much new information an audience can comprehend all at once.

You might want to ask some colleagues to check your presentation beforehand. Explain the message that you are trying to convey (the goal of the presentation) and get feedback from your colleagues about the content of the presentation and the amount of information being presented.

2.   Use words to explain your analysis results.

Analysts tend to explain the analysis results with numbers, using a lot of technical jargon that laymen are not familiar with. Your explanation may sound very boring to some people. If your objective is to make your audience understand what you are saying, to take action and approve your idea, then <u>your real focus should not be on showing the analysis results themselves but rather on processing the results to suit your objective and effectively speak to your audience (e.g. explaining your intention with words instead).</u>

I often see analysts showing data *as it is*, using a lot of graphs in the presentation, which tends to drive the audience away.

Fig. 6-3 Translate the analysis results into words

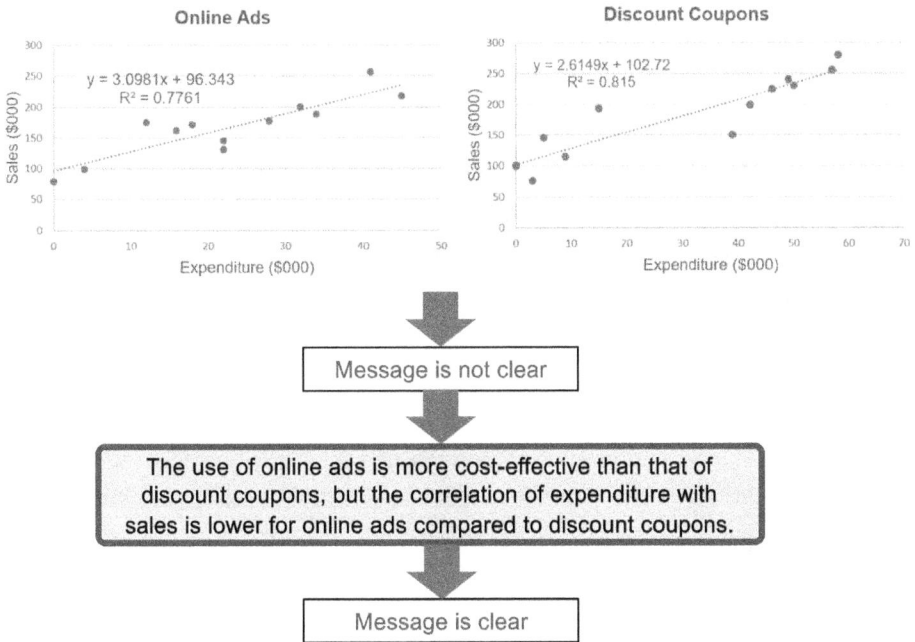

Online Ads

y = 3.0981x + 96.343
R² = 0.7761

Sales ($000)
Expenditure ($000)

Discount Coupons

y = 2.6149x + 102.72
R² = 0.815

Sales ($000)
Expenditure ($000)

Message is not clear

The use of online ads is more cost-effective than that of discount coupons, but the correlation of expenditure with sales is lower for online ads compared to discount coupons.

Message is clear

In these cases, using brief sentences to explain the key takeaways from the analysis results is far more effective in conveying your message.

In **Figure 6-3**, for example, don't you think the message is far clearer after being provided with the summary sentence rather than just being told to compare the two analysis results?

There is another advantage in summarizing the analysis results with words.

Analysts often focus on obtaining analysis results and forget their real objective—to determine the kind of message they want to convey, and the kind of information necessary to convey that message.

My advice for you is to make a habit of giving an interpretation to each analysis result. By checking whether your analysis results help you reach your real goal, you will not lose track, and you can use the interpretation notes to create your message when you finalize your presentation.

3.   Cite your sources to prove that your analysis results are reliable.

Although this may be obvious, I want to emphasize how important it is to cite your sources.

Analysts often collect and utilize data which is available to the public, such as data from the internet, but both good and bad data are in a hopeless jumble, and not all data is reliable. Even if your analysis is perfect, the fact that your data is from an unreliable source will make your argument less convincing, and all your hard work will go to waste.

To avoid making such a rookie mistake, <u>cite the source of your information at all times</u>.

Officially recognized sources are usually more reliable (public institutions, organizations, etc.). Reliability is crucial. Once your audience sees the sources and are reassured, they will not doubt the sources' reliability. Otherwise, your audience would get distracted and might not listen to you.

Even when I am done collecting all the essential data for analysis, I still like to search for any public data that I can use.

You can still share some data that is not officially recognized. Citing the source of information is a sign of good faith. It is common sense (a prerequisite) in the academic world.

What I have just explained may be too obvious, but try looking for citations in presentation materials created by others. You may doubt whether some cited sources are accurate. Some people even forget citations.

Thus, giving an accurate source for your information will help your presentation stand out amongst the others.

Visualize data in addition to displaying numbers!

I mentioned how important it is to summarize your analysis results with words. Similarly, your audience will have a much better understanding of the results when it is visualized in addition to being expressed in numerical values.

Charts and graphs are the most common visualization tools in data analysis. You can find many books on how to utilize Excel to create graphs from data, so I'll skip that part. Instead, I'll share other key points about visualization.

Describe the entire data set with a graph.

When you aggregate the characteristics of data with a statistical indicator, the characteristics of each data point cannot be seen. In general, an audience tends to feel reassured when they are shown a complete picture. They may feel frustrated when they are only provided with a processed analysis result (especially high-ranking staff). As I mentioned, though, make sure that you focus on the most important message that you want to convey, and don't show excessive data for no tangible reason.

Graphs such as histograms (see Chapter 3) are efficient and effective in visualizing the entire data set.

Fig. 6-4 Showing the analysis results with a histogram

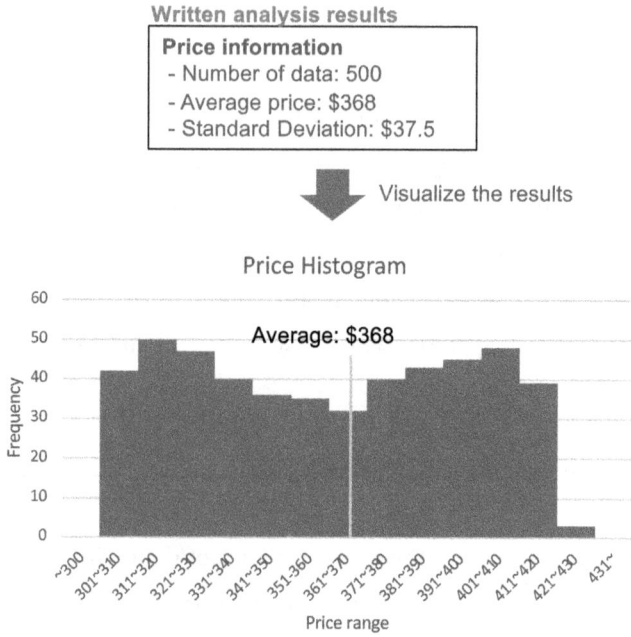

Written analysis results

Price information
- Number of data: 500
- Average price: $368
- Standard Deviation: $37.5

Visualize the results

Price Histogram

In **Figure 6-4**, the written analysis results summarize the characteristics of the data set, but it is difficult to imagine what the entire data set looks like. On the other hand, the histogram gives you an image of the whole data set. I am not concluding that there is only one superior or correct answer, but I think histograms describe the entire data set for an audience a lot better than a written summary.

Use speech bubbles to emphasize key points.

Once you visualize data with a graph, don't just stop there. Your argument should be supported by both graphs and sentences. Write down key sentences (make them brief) in your presentation and highlight them with arrows and speech bubbles to captivate your audience's attention.

Fig. 6-5 Adding your conclusion/message

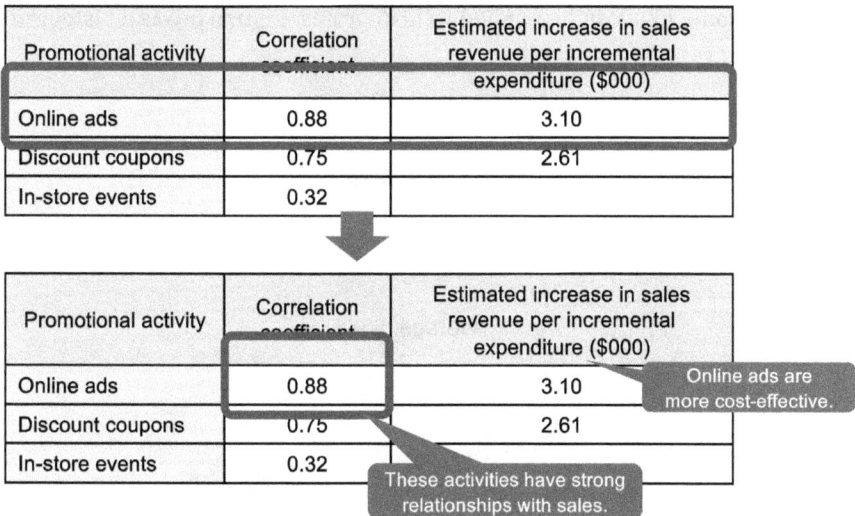

Promotional activity	Correlation coefficient	Estimated increase in sales revenue per incremental expenditure ($000)
Online ads	0.88	3.10
Discount coupons	0.75	2.61
In-store events	0.32	

Promotional activity	Correlation coefficient	Estimated increase in sales revenue per incremental expenditure ($000)
Online ads	0.88	3.10
Discount coupons	0.75	2.61
In-store events	0.32	

Online ads are more cost-effective.

These activities have strong relationships with sales.

This time, I used charts to describe the analysis results (**Figure 6-5**). The first chart summarizes Alex's correlation and regression analyses. It is a simple and concise comparison of the results.

On the other hand, the second chart emphasizes the key message that the speaker wants to get across to the audience. Again, I'm not saying that there is only one correct answer, but it's a good idea to change your chart depending on your objective or audience to deliver your message more effectively.

For instance, if I'm just reviewing information with my colleagues, I would show the first chart and tell them the key points as I go through the presentation. At this stage, I don't want to give a conclusion as it could limit the exchange of any new ideas.

However, the second chart comes in handy when I already have a conclusion and want an executive to understand and approve my proposal, especially when there are too many discussion topics and a very limited amount of time for decision making.

Therefore, you can think of it this way: how one chooses to display data is a *strategy* to convey your message and motivate your audience.

The same idea can be applied to histograms. **Figure 6-6** is a histogram in which key points are highlighted for an audience.

Fig. 6-6 Adding a Message to the Histogram

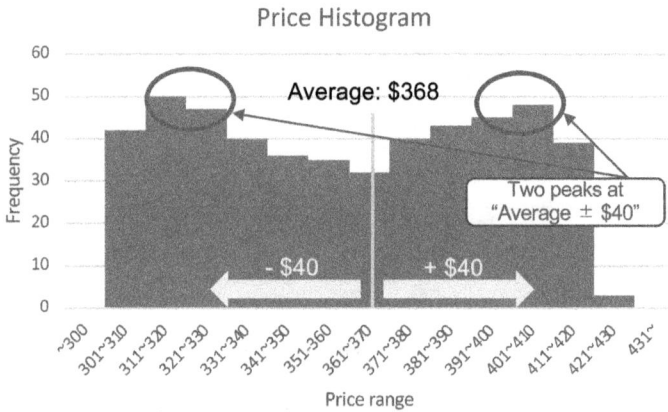

Price Histogram

A histogram is useful in showing an overview of the whole data set, but what is observed and learned from it varies between each audience member. In Figure 6-6, some people may find that the scope of variance between $300 and $420 is quite large ($120). Others may get the impression that prices are low by looking at the most frequent price range ($311 to $320).

There is a lot of information, and there are several focal points in an entire data set. By highlighting the main points in your presentation, you can make sure that your audience does not receive irrelevant messages or misunderstand what you are trying to say.

Please observe how other people get creative in their presentations, and develop new ways of highlighting key information.

Emphasize key points by using comparisons.

Showing your own data is not the only way to share information. You can emphasize your message by **comparing your own data with other data**.

In **Figure 6-7**, the first histogram shows the price data from one company. Although you can learn a lot from this histogram, you can also compare this data with that of a competitor to highlight a large difference in the data, as shown in the second histogram. If this difference is linked to the message that you are trying to convey, this type of graph is a great tool to bring out the key points in your argument.

Fig. 6-7 Highlighting by comparison

Sales price distribution - our company

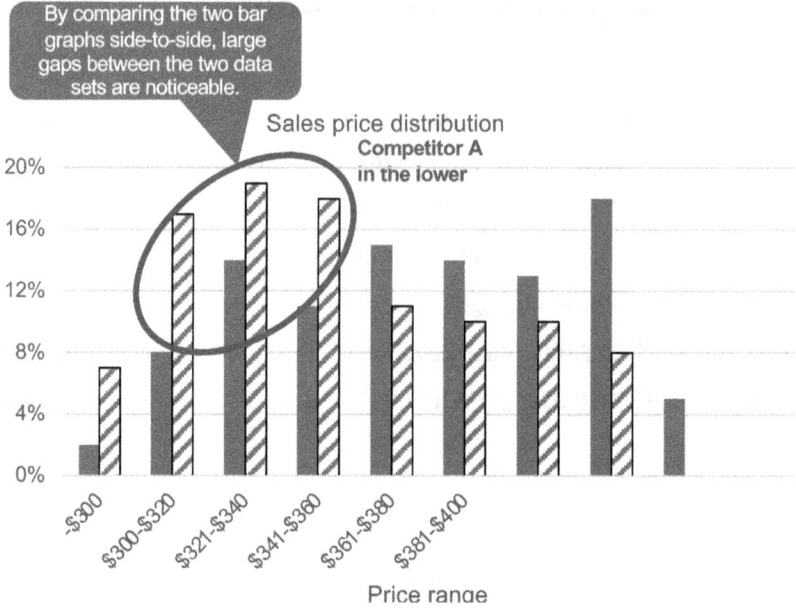

By comparing the two bar graphs side-to-side, large gaps between the two data sets are noticeable.

Sales price distribution

Competitor A in the lower

Price range

The second histogram shows the price data of a competitor (Competitor A) in the same market in addition to the initial data. The two datum are placed next to each other for a relative comparison. Thus, the difference is highlighted.

Depending on the message that you want to convey, you could draw different conclusions from this graph: that Competitor A has lower pricing; or that our products sell relatively well, even with higher pricing. In general, though, isn't it easier to deliver a message using comparable data?

There are other ways to compare data as well. As I mentioned in Chapter 1, you can use different attributes such as time, region, customer (age, gender, income, industry, the size of the organization, preferences, etc.). For example, you can use the time attribute to compare data with that of the previous year or month. You can also use the region attribute to compare the difference in data in each sales territory or country.

Use the same attribute to compare data.

Please remember that you need to **use the same attribute to compare data**. In Figure 6-7, for example, if you switch the sales frequency ratio on the y-axis to the number of data instead, and if the total number of samples is different for each company, the populations are different, so there is no point in comparing the numbers. That is why I converted the numbers to the same attribute—the ratio (%) out of the populations.

There are many ways to display data, depending on the speaker's ideas and creativity. Just make sure not to overdo it, as that would make the presentation less impactful.

> ## Revisit your hypothesis at the end.

You are finally at the last step of an analysis. We went through the following steps. Do you remember the hypothesis approach that I described in the beginning?

1. Prepare necessary data based on your hypothesis (Preface, Chapter 1).
2. Choose your analysis method and repeat the analysis through trial and error (Chapters 2 to 5).
3. Interpret your analysis results (Chapters 2 to 5).
4. Think of ways to clearly convey your conclusion (Chapter 6).

In the final step, you should check whether your objective (goal) has remained consistent while you progressed through Steps 1 to 4. In other words, **does the output in Step 4 provide an answer to the hypothesis in Step 1?**

You can easily lose track of your initial hypothesis while you are analyzing. The output at the end may be logical, but when you look back at the initial hypothesis, the output may not necessarily answer your initial question. Thus, in the final stage, you need to re-check, and if you lost track, go back to the point where you veered off track in order to reinforce your logic. To avoid analyzing all over again, though, it is more ideal to **revisit your initial objective and hypothesis during each step.**

COLUMN: USE A PARETO CHART TO NARROW DOWN THE AMOUNT OF INFORMATION.

Having collected a lot of data, you may need to narrow it down in the end. Here's a guide to how you can narrow down the scope of data depending on the degree of priority or influence.

Fig. 6-8 Creating a Pareto chart

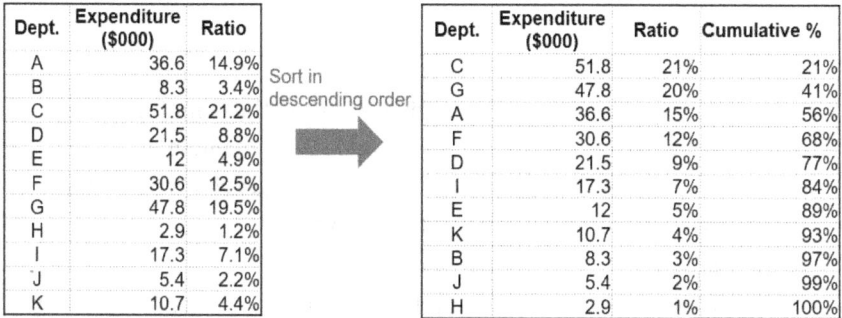

Dept.	Expenditure ($000)	Ratio
A	36.6	14.9%
B	8.3	3.4%
C	51.8	21.2%
D	21.5	8.8%
E	12	4.9%
F	30.6	12.5%
G	47.8	19.5%
H	2.9	1.2%
I	17.3	7.1%
J	5.4	2.2%
K	10.7	4.4%

Sort in descending order →

Dept.	Expenditure ($000)	Ratio	Cumulative %
C	51.8	21%	21%
G	47.8	20%	41%
A	36.6	15%	56%
F	30.6	12%	68%
D	21.5	9%	77%
I	17.3	7%	84%
E	12	5%	89%
K	10.7	4%	93%
B	8.3	3%	97%
J	5.4	2%	99%
H	2.9	1%	100%

Figure 6-8 shows this year's expenditure data from different departments in a company (A to K). Say, your goal for next year is to cut costs as much as possible, and you are trying to identify excessive spending from this data.

If you want to analyze the data efficiently and prioritize the most important data to show your audience, it is a bad idea to look into the details of every single department and give that information straight to your audience.

Pareto charts are useful in this kind of situation because it sorts data in descending order and specifies the scope of data that seems relevant. A Pareto chart helps you explain why you chose a particular scope of data from an objective point of view on the basis that the largest value is the most prioritized or influential information.

Although sorting data in descending order sounds awfully simple, it is a very reliable and convincing method for explaining why you chose a particular scope of data.

The y-axis does not always have to be an absolute value. In some cases, you should compare data on a per unit basis (e.g. per unit area, per capita, etc.). For example, it doesn't make any sense to compare the amount of expenditures of two companies if the number of employees in each company is entirely different. In that case, you need to adjust the data of expenditure to "per employee".

To make a Pareto chart (See Figure 6-8), first, you need to sort your data (in this case, this year's expenditure) in descending order (The SORT function in Excel comes in handy). Then, calculate the ratio (%) of each value to the total sum, and the cumulative percentage.

Lastly, use the original data to create a bar graph, and the cumulative percentage to create a line graph. Here are the procedures for Excel 2019 (Procedures may vary depending on the version of your Excel.):

1. Create a bar graph with the original data and the cumulative percentage. Then, right-click the bars for the cumulative percentage.
2. Select "Change Chart Type" to switch the bar graph to a line graph.
3. Choose the chart type ("Line") for the cumulative percentage data series and check the "Secondary Axis" check-box. Press "OK."
4. You're all done. The completed Pareto chart is shown in Figure 6-9.

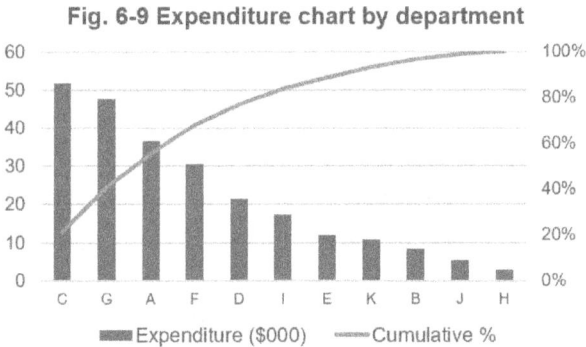

Fig. 6-9 Expenditure chart by department

The cumulative percentage is necessary to determine the scope of data needed for an analysis or a presentation. In this case, I set a premise that the company can effectively cut spending by a great amount if they focus on the top 60% (You can only cut a small amount in the departments with less expenditure). Therefore, I concluded that I will focus on cutting spending in the first four departments (C, G, A and F).

By limiting the scope of analysis to these four departments, I was able to simplify the amount of work and the amount of information in my presentation.

Epilogue

Alex nearly gave up many times before his boss approved of his presentation material.

A day before the deadline, the manager also gave him an approval. Alex managed to e-mail the finalized presentation material to the executive office after a long day's work just as everyone started going home.

Alex's Presentation Material:

New Market Entry Plan (Country X)

Date: mm/dd/yyyy

Market Outline

Country X has a larger population % of younger people with high sales potential.

Population: XXXX
Age distribution: ----
GDP: $XXXX
Income distribution: ----
Culture, Religion: ----
Purchase trend: ----

Age group distribution (Country X)

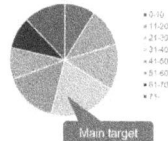

- 0-10
- 11-20
- 21-30
- 31-40
- 41-50
- 51-60
- 61-70
- 71-

Main target

Summary

(1) **Conclusions drawn from analysis**
   - If we enter this market (Country X), annual sales revenue will increase by approx. $33M.
   - Identified some effective measures to mitigate sales risks
   - Target sales revenue can be achieved within the first year.
   (Positive NPV in 5 years)

(2) **Proposal**
   - Early entry into the Country X market
   - Officially authorize the plan for the next year

Market Size   \<Ch. 2\>

Country X will be our 3rd highest market share (20%) next year

Revenue share estimation

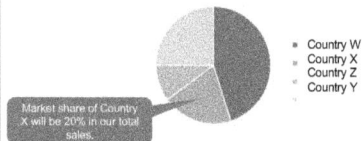

- Country W
- Country X
- Country Z
- Country Y

Market share of Country X will be 20% in our total sales.

Pricing strategy and sales plan

Estimated sales variance risk: ±11%   <Ch. 3>

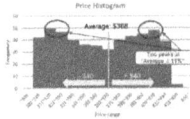

Estimated total sales revenue:
$33M
Risk range: $28M ~ $36.5M

($M)	1st year	2nd year	3rd year	4th year	5th year
Sales revenue	30.0	32.1	34.5	36.8	42.0

Profit estimation

NPV* will be positive in 5 years

($M)	1st year	2nd year	3rd year	4th year	5th year
Operating profit	7.6	7.8	8.1	10.2	12.4

Our goal in the current business plan
will be achieved in the 1st year

*NPV: Net Present Value

Sales strategy and expenditure plan

Identified two effective sales activities   <Ch. 4,5>

Promotional activity	Correlation coefficient	Estimated revenue increase per incremental expenditure ($000)
Online ads	0.86	3.10
Discount coupons	0.75	2.61
In-store events	0.32	

Expenditure plan ($000)	Q1	Q2	Q3	Q4
Online ads	20	25	25	32
Discount coupons	40	30	25	20

Conclusion

- If we enter this market (Country X), annual sales revenue will increase by approx. $33M (±11%).
- Effective measures to mitigate the sale risks are identified
- Current profit plan will be achieved in the 1st year (NPV will also be positive in 5 years)

What to do Next

(i)   Enter into an agreement with a local sales partner
(ii) Start training local sales representatives
(iii) Continue research to gain more detailed market insights

Alex reflected upon the entire project. Alex and his boss started off the discussion with a bird's eye view on the whole market and then looked into each sales strategy. This flow of information, first looking at the big picture and then looking into the details, was very smooth and logical.

Alex's mind and body felt exhausted, but he was finally at ease. He felt less nervous after studying the basics of analysis. Overall, he was satisfied and confident that his skills to utilize numerical data to make a business plan improved significantly from a few weeks ago.

The next morning, Alex's boss spoke to him.

Boss: "Good morning, Alex. I checked the email you sent to the executive office. Good job!"

Alex: "Thanks, boss! I'm glad I met the deadline, but I'm still worried about whether it was good enough."

Boss: "Well, there's no such thing as a perfect plan. I also get nervous when I do presentations."

Alex: "Really? You always look so confident."

Boss: "Oh, of course. Your attitude is also a key to success. Your confidence level can affect the quality of your presentation."

Alex: "I see. I learned so much from this project. At first, 'statistics' gave me an impression that anyone can reach the needed answers right away after learning the methods and logic behind it. Now I know that there's no correct answer in data analysis. You can get creative in many ways!"

Boss: "I think you did a good job! Please remember—the methods I taught you this time are not necessarily useful in any other situation. You need to observe other people's output and experience more trial and error. Keep practicing!"

"Also, you should go back to the beginning and think of a better hypothesis that would lead you to the output. Review the key points so that you can do a more efficient and effective analysis in your next project."

Alex: "I will!"

Alex read his notes and reviewed the procedures he took to draw a structural diagram.

Analysis Structure (Alex's Example)

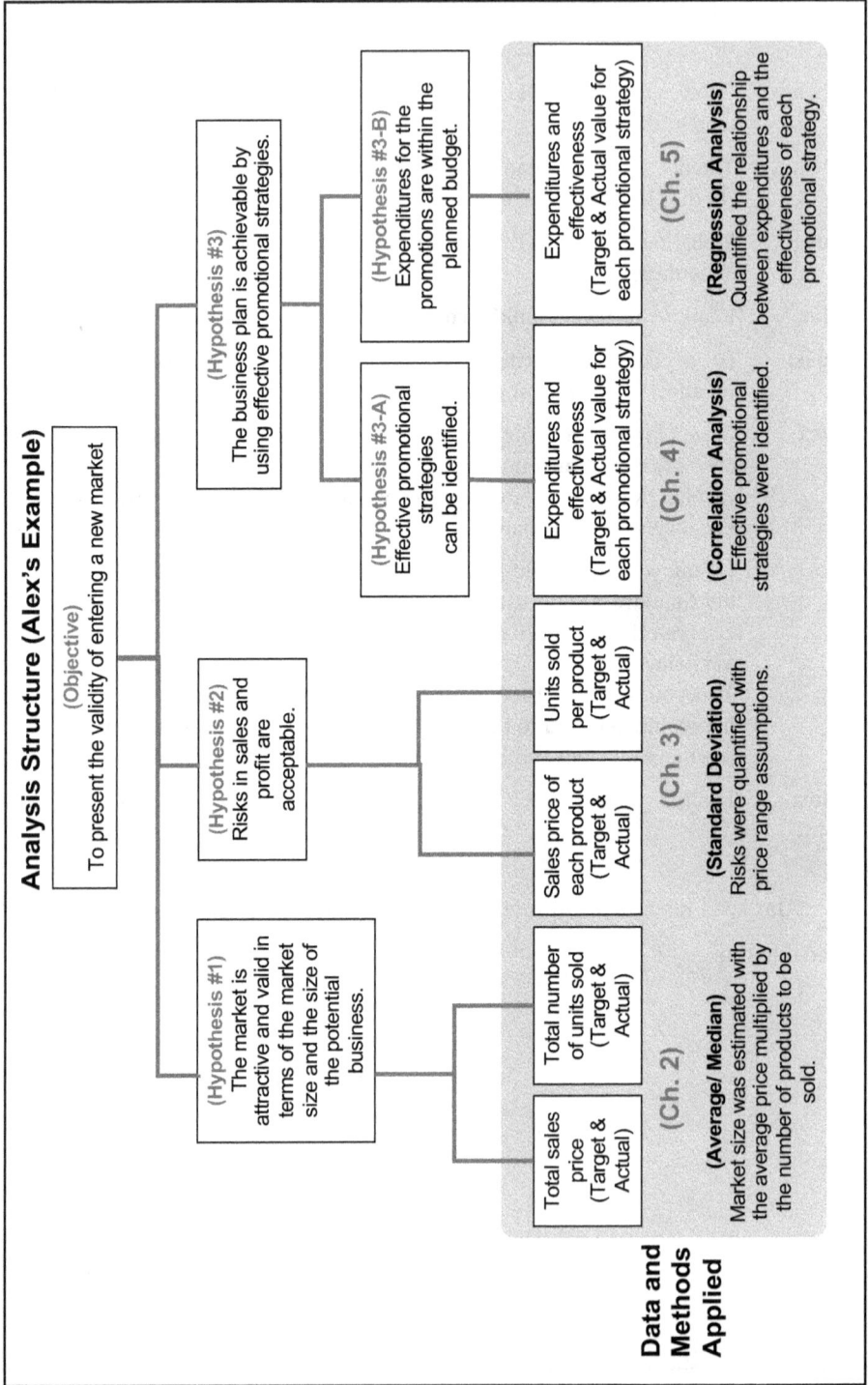

(Objective)
To present the validity of entering a new market

(Hypothesis #1)
The market is attractive and valid in terms of the market size and the size of the potential business.

Total sales price (Target & Actual)

Total number of units sold (Target & Actual)

(Ch. 2)

(Average/ Median)
Market size was estimated with the average price multiplied by the number of products to be sold.

(Hypothesis #2)
Risks in sales and profit are acceptable.

Sales price of each product (Target & Actual)

Units sold per product (Target & Actual)

(Ch. 3)

(Standard Deviation)
Risks were quantified with price range assumptions.

(Hypothesis #3)
The business plan is achievable by using effective promotional strategies.

(Hypothesis #3-A)
Effective promotional strategies can be identified.

Expenditures and effectiveness (Target & Actual value for each promotional strategy)

(Ch. 4)

(Correlation Analysis)
Effective promotional strategies were identified.

(Hypothesis #3-B)
Expenditures for the promotions are within the planned budget.

Expenditures and effectiveness (Target & Actual value for each promotional strategy)

(Ch. 5)

(Regression Analysis)
Quantified the relationship between expenditures and the effectiveness of each promotional strategy.

Data and Methods Applied

Alex: "Ah, it's easier to understand the theory when you make a structural diagram."

Alex's Boss came back.

Boss: "I forgot to give you the heads up. I spoke with the manager. We think you're ready to do this presentation on your own. Make sure you get some practice!"

Alex didn't see this coming because he thought someone else would lead the presentation.

Boss: "The executive staff of business planning will join our meeting. They're really looking forward to your presentation. Don't worry, you've got this!"

Alex felt nervous, but he wanted to overcome his fear of giving a presentation in the same way that he just conquered his fear of statistical analysis.

Alex: "Okay. I can do this!"

Discussion and Concluding Remarks

In data analysis, I have often encountered people who confuse data utilization at the corporate level (i.e. sophisticated statistics, data science and big data) and data utilization by businesspeople at an individual level. I hope that this book helped you realize that businesspeople do not necessarily need to master "statistics" or "data science" in order to utilize data and achieve their goals.

In this book, I focused only on the most practical methods of data analysis that can be easily applied in our day-to-day business. I introduced not only the methods, but also a specific case in which each method was incorporated to tell a story (draw a conclusion). My objective is to show you the advantages and disadvantages of each method and the way of thinking to apply them in real life. Sometimes, each method can be used individually. In general, however, it is much more effective to use multiple methods that complement each other and strengthen your argument, or storytelling.

"What are the grounds of your argument?"

I asked this question in the Japanese title of this book. Whether you are making a business plan or presentation, you need to be prepared to answer this question.

As I mentioned, data and the soft skills to utilize data will help you reach the answer.

I have been teaching how to develop such soft skills in schools, companies and other organizations. Many of my clients are well-read in statistics or data analysis, but still struggle to utilize data and reach their goals. Once they learn how to use soft skills, it gets so much easier!

This book is currently a best seller and widely read by businesspeople in Japan. It has been published in Asia in various languages, and will continue to assist many people with real world applications of data.

I decided to publish an English version as well because I strongly believe that data is a global tool without any barriers, and its power can be unleashed no matter where you are.

I truly hope that this book will assist many of you who are struggling to apply your knowledge from a countless number of statistics and data science textbooks to real life to reach your goals.

Feel free to contact me at any time if you need any guidance or support.

I would like to give a special thanks to my loving and supportive family: my wife Akiko, my son Yuki and my daughter Tomoka. I love you.

Author Bio

Name of Author: Yoshiki Kashiwagi

Founder and CEO of Data & Story LLC (Japan). A graduate of Emory University's Goizueta Business School (MBA) and the Science and Technology Department at Keio University (Bachelor's Degree), Mr. Kashiwagi has had experience working at Hitachi, Ltd. and Nissan Motor Co., Ltd. He joined Nissan in 2004, and became a manager of Global Marketing & Sales and the Business Transformation Group. Mr. Kashiwagi has worked as a project leader, utilizing data analysis strategically in starting new businesses and analyzing, assessing and improving the company's work flow in global business. In October, 2014, he started his new business as a data analysis advisor and a training expert. Using his business experience, Mr. Kashiwagi has been teaching seminars for his corporate clients on problem solving and analysis skills that can be used in real-life business situations. Mr. Kashiwagi is also a Visiting Professor at Tama Graduate School of Business, teaching part-time at Yokohama National University.

Data & Story LLC: https://www.data-story.net/english
LinkedIn: https://www.linkedin.com/in/business-data-analysis

www.ingramcontent.com/pod-product-compliance
Lightning Source LLC
Chambersburg PA
CBHW050505210326
41521CB00011B/2330